MIKA
HAKKINEN

As part of our ongoing market research, we are always pleased to receive
comments about our books, suggestions for new titles, or requests for catalogues.
Please write to: The Editorial Director, Haynes Publishing, Sparkford, Nr Yeovil,
Somerset BA22 7JJ.

MIKA
HAKKINEN
Doing what comes naturally

CHRISTOPHER HILTON

Haynes

First published in July 1997

British Library Cataloguing in Publication Data:
A catalogue record for this book is
available from the British Library

ISBN 1 85960 402 1

Library of Congress catalog card no. 97-70201

Published by Haynes Publishing, Sparkford,
Nr Yeovil, Somerset, BA22 7JJ UK.

Haynes Publishing Inc., 861 Lawrence Drive,
Newbury Park, California 91320, USA.

Designed & typeset by G&M, Raunds, Northamptonshire
Printed and bound in France by Imprimerie Pollina s.a., Luçon, France n°72408

Contents

Acknowledgements

PRIMARY THANKS TO Mika Hakkinen himself for giving generously of his time in Monaco and providing (mostly!) candid answers to a host of questions that seemed impertinent or invasive. I wanted to cajole him into discussing the shadowland of Formula 1 – the places rarely explored – as well as the action, because he is not like most drivers in perception, philosophy or the way he conducts his life. He was extremely eloquent about the mental and physical aspects of driving, and the consequences. More than this, he showed me how to spell Pekka Pirkola, which might not seem much to you, but (in the face of the impossible Finnish language) remains a particular comfort. You'll see.

His manager, Keke Rosberg, was instrumental in broadening the scope of the book, and Keke's sister Jatta made things happen. Another member of that team, Didier Coton, went at gathering pictures like a terrier. I'm particularly gratified that Hakkinen's parents raided the family album to provide the early photographs, which are a delight.

A Finnish journalist, Erkki Mustakari, has known Hakkinen from the beginning of his career as an international single-seater driver and recounted those times with relish. He was also kind enough to conduct an interview with Hakkinen's parents, which has made the book more complete than it could conceivably have been otherwise.

I am also indebted to Peter Collins, who tried valiantly to run and save Team Lotus; Tony Dodgins of *F1 Racing* magazine for active assistance; Dick Bennetts of West Surrey Racing for so many candid and affectionate memories; Suzanne Radbone, formerly of West Surrey Racing and Team Lotus, for all her insights, honesty and integrity; and

Anita Smith, Julian Bailey, Otto Rensing, Allan McNish, Hughie Absalom, John Alcorn, Mika Sohlberg, the very same Pekka Pirkola, Mark Blundell, Antti Puskala; Corinne Vasserfallen of Sauber; Wilfred Muller of Porsche. Doctors Stephen Lewis of the Flinders Medical Centre, South Australia, and Jerome Cockings of the Princess Alexandra Hospital, Brisbane, have a very special place because without them neither the subject of this book nor, as a direct consequence, the book would exist.

In a different but no less important way, thanks to Simon Taylor, Chairman of Haymarket Specialist Motoring Publications Limited, for permission to quote from *Autosport* and *Motoring News*; Bob Jennings of *The Advertiser*, Adelaide, for providing that newspaper's coverage of the crash of 1995; and Mark Burgess for permission to quote from *Karting magazine*.

I have leaned on the compendious and comprehensive *Grand Prix Data Book* by David Hayhoe and David Holland (Duke) for definitive reference, and the *Marlboro Grand Prix Guide* for quick information about the facts, figures and decimal points.

Please note, and this is important, that there are three Mikas in this book: Hakkinen, Salo and Sohlberg. For simplicity, and to keep you sane until the end, whenever you read just 'Mika' by itself it refers to Hakkinen. Cleverly, I call Salo 'Salo' and Sohlberg 'Sohlberg'.

Jatta asked me what sort of a book it was going to be ('not nasty, I hope'), and I said it'll be honest. More, it is intended to be the story of an evolution: from a shy young fellow – of modest means, raised in a faraway place, speaking the impossible language and nothing else – to the worldly, wealthy and wise (truly!) man you see today, who is one of the best drivers in the world, no question; and one of the most popular, too.

Straight
from the grid

THAT NOVEMBER MORNING the blond, fresh-faced young man woke from a sleep of very great depth because sedation had been withdrawn some hours before. Mika Hakkinen's eyes scanned the room and he understood that he was in hospital. He didn't know it was the Royal Adelaide Hospital: he couldn't know that. A doctor – Stephen Lewis – leaned over him, monitoring. Hakkinen lifted a hand and manipulated two fingers across his chest, mimicking human motion. Mute, he was asking – perhaps beseeching – Lewis to tell him whether he could still walk. Lewis realised intuitively that Hakkinen would draw a single conclusion: *if I can still walk, I can still drive racing cars.* Lewis responded with a mute but completely international gesture of his own: thumbs up. A slow smile spread across Hakkinen's face and he sank back into the sleep of very great depth.

And that was Saturday, 11 November 1995.

Hakkinen has no proper memory of the moving fingers, although that somebody else says he did it does not surprise him. All of it remains distorted, tortured, a wild storm and a great calm. When I explain what Lewis says, Hakkinen insists that his – Hakkinen's – primary purpose must surely have been to know if he would be able to walk again, the driving secondary.

Hmmm.

The day before seemed literally a lifetime away, and was. In qualifying for the Australian Grand Prix, Hakkinen was coming down Rundle Road, a gully of a place because the walls on either side had the effect of narrowing it, steepening it. He pushed the McLaren up towards 250kph, which is goddamned quick in metric or imperial –

155mph, give or take. The walls, and the tall stooping trees behind them, flicked by with a gathering urgency.

Just up ahead, like a jaw opening, Rundle Road turned hard right into the long Brabham Straight. This turning was called Brewery Bend, one side of a triangle where three roads met. In the context of a street racing circuit, the triangle represented a broad, open expanse of tarmac. In the context of a Formula 1 car preparing to brake from the 250kph to 170kph – the 155mph to 105mph, give or take – in a matter of metres, it represented the best run-off area you could expect, up to and including a tyre wall along the far angle.

As the ferocious brakes of the McLaren dug into the speed, Hakkinen changed down to fifth gear and placed the car over to the left, exploiting the width of the track. That made his passage through the right-hander – lasting half a second – smoother, easier, faster, bang, bang, bang.

The jaw opened more and more. His gloved hands had begun to turn the steering wheel into the corner. Without warning the car broke free, snapped completely from his control. The right front tyre hung off the ground. The rear left had picked up debris, puncturing it and destroying the whole balance of the car.

By reflex Hakkinen churned the steering wheel left-left-left, his arms intertwined, wrestling to regain control. The car had already reached the apex of the corner, but *sideways*. His arms churned the steering wheel again, but the car had slewed and was travelling *backwards*.

The car reached kerbing painted red, yellow and blue and the slope of this kerbing launched it a metre into the air. It screamed towards the tyre wall like a stone skimming a pond and, as it went, bounced three times. Each bounce drew a gasp of smoke from the right front tyre and laid a scar of burnished rubber on the surface of the road. By the third bounce it had rotated to be *forwards* again. A great, centrifugal, geometrical force held it and manipulated it. Hakkinen was completely helpless.

The car rammed the tyre wall virtually head on at 200kph – 125mph, give or take.

The impact, the sheer centrifugal force, was so extreme that it plundered Hakkinen's head downwards until it smote the steering wheel a terrible instantaneous blow. That fractured his skull. His head came back up and thrashed from side to side, the force now manipulating even this. He was conscious, but his mouth clamped shut. Within two or three minutes lack of oxygen would produce brain damage. A very few minutes after that, lack of oxygen would be fatal.

The radio crackled to life in the medical car, a white estate, parked a hundred metres away, over there to the left behind the Armco barrier. The rear doors were open, as they always deliberately were: for speed of access, just in case. The two doctors standing beside it slipped in and within 15 seconds were at the McLaren. One was Lewis, the other Jerome Cockings. By then the first of the three marshals behind the tyre wall had clambered over and was attending to the most immediate tasks. Three fire-fighters had positioned themselves at the rear of the McLaren.

What followed was a virtually perfect demonstration of anticipation, preparation and employing received knowledge. Hakkinen did not suffer brain damage, much less die.

And life went on as before, give or take.

Hakkinen recovered so completely that, a mere four months later, he was able to compete in the opening race of the following season – Melbourne, a sort of return to the scene, if you know what I mean. He had a queasy feeling when the plane passed on to Australian soil and he thought *yes, this is the country where it happened*. He qualified on the third row of the grid and finished fifth, his mind and body able to tolerate 1 hour 34 minutes 25.562 seconds of Grand Prix intensity. That was partly because driving at speed had always come naturally to him.

Interesting. He was the most untypical of Grand Prix drivers, who seemed to live somewhere on the other side of laid-back. When he was with Lotus he moved into a house at Wymondham without telling his friend – who was renting it – that he was going to do so. Just turned up one Sunday night with his gear. *Everything'll be fine – what's the problem?* This attitude, or approach, to being alive infuriated some and enchanted others. (He disputes the accuracy of the moving-in 'incident', but was smiling coyly when he disputed it.)

The central core of his life was driving, just driving, as it had been since he was six when, on his first lap in a hired go-kart, he rolled it comprehensively. He didn't think *I have survived*; no, when his alarmed father ran up he thought *I must be careful because this can frighten other people but it's great. I must get a go-kart of my own.*

And life went on, give or take, all the way to February 1997, when he confronted his most important season. He had yet to win a Grand Prix, and McLaren, once the team to beat, had not won a race since – aye – Adelaide in 1993. Hakkinen would be carrying a lot of weight, his and other people's.

McLaren had a new sponsor, the West cigarette company of Germany, who decided to celebrate the launch of the 1997 car and its Mercedes engine by hiring Alexandra Palace – a vast venue – in North London and having a pop concert there. Apart from the car, the evening offered the singing of a group called the Spice Girls – who were very much in vogue – and attracted over 5,000 people. Hakkinen and his team-mate David Coulthard went up on the stage with the Spice Girls, kissed them for the cameras, then unveiled the car. The 5,000 high-clapped their approval, strobe lighting pulsed and Hakkinen beamed benignly on the whole thing while the sport that had so often been closest to show business melted effortlessly into the dubious embrace of show business itself.

Mika Hakkinen moves towards third place in the Australian Grand Prix 1997, and he'd never been driving better (ICN U.K. Bureau).

There must be something about Hakkinen and Australia, because Melbourne the second time round was next. Coulthard won, Hakkinen third, and the communal relief between them was so profound that Hakkinen picked Coulthard clean off the ground, hoisted him high and shook him as if he was a bottle of champagne.

And life went on, through Brazil and Argentina and the misnomer of the San Marino Grand Prix at Imola. At this point I journeyed to Monaco for a serious in-depth ask-what-you-want meaning-of-life (give or take) meeting with Hakkinen at Rosberg's office in Monaco. Without making this a travelogue, let me explain that street numbers in the Principality are even more sporadic than anywhere you've ever been, and a much better way to find the office is simply to shout 'Rosberg!' at anyone within ear-shot. I tried this in (what turned out to be) a nearby bank and a clerk pointed the way.

'Rosberg, over there, *that* door – not the other door.'

A foyer shimmering with what seemed to be dark marble polished like ice, a sigh of a lift inhaling as it rose, a crisp surgical-clean corridor, then a whole corner of the tenth floor behind closed doors; a reception area where the walls are shimmering with action pictures of Rosberg and Hakkinen and another Finnish driver – JJ Lehto – who, in one picture, is standing behind a nubile woman with breasts like Alps stretching and straining her blouse. JJ's eyes are rolling wondrously at this panoramic view, and I say *let's have the picture in the book, let's caption it Two Good Friends*, but Rosberg's sister Jatta isn't having any of that.

No.

That's what she said.

Hakkinen comes along, easy and loose and natural and unforced. He moves crisply, however, and is entirely unafraid to be alive: that is to say, entirely unafraid to be what he is and no faint attempt to be anything else. Not give or take, not even take it or leave it, *I'm me*. He spends a laborious amount of time scanning and sifting the photographs his parents have sent ('Haven't seen these for many years'), giving the background to each, adding a background touch or two to each.

There's a restaurant on the third floor and we go down. The lift sighs

Opposite The mature racer, preparing (Photo Wilhelm, courtesy Mercedes-Benz).

again at the same softened pitch, and during the descent I recount how the photographer Antti Puskala was once on the Underground in London with another Finn and they found themselves pressed in the rush-hour crush against two very attractive ladies. Puskala said – in Finnish, so completely safe – the sort of thing a chap might say to another chap about very attractive ladies. The attractive ladies were Finnair hostesses . . .

The lift landed, Hakkinen and I are walking through yet another foyer to the restaurant and he recounts how the completely safe can turn out to be even worse than Puskala's purgatory. Hakkinen and a friend had been gently deriding someone at a neighbouring table in another restaurant – as it transpired, someone preparing to go on missionary work or some such – and the missionary deliberately let the deriding go on and on and on in silence, then rose, said monotone and ordinary in Finnish the equivalent of *have a nice day*, and departed.

As we walk Hakkinen feels the shock and humiliation living again, the whole of it, vivid and rearing horribly from a basic human pit of transgression that will never go away. I want you to know that the anecdote doesn't amount to much of itself – we all blunder – but it does amount to a great deal when it is volunteered by a millionaire in Monaco who is happy to demonstrate his own vulnerability and, equally, is uninterested in pretence. *I'm me.* After many years of writing about this sort of thing I am persuaded that only big men sincerely tell true stories against themselves, and do so for the most natural, uncalculated reason. The stories are true, part of themselves, *me.*

At lunch we settle down to talk his career through. Mika Hakkinen is lively company, amusing, perceptive, expressive, occasionally introspective, rarely reluctant to discuss what happened and why. When he's in the mood, he wields words by wringing the meaning he wants out of them, and certain words, which he makes sound racy, will soon become old favourites in the narrative of this story: *loved* doing something, *professional* as in the proper way things should be done, *mega* attached to almost anything for emphasis, *fantastic* to catch his mood, and, frequently, *crazy* to mean nicely mad, not clinically mad. In short, conversation can become like a qualifying lap – and from the beginning he's been good at qualifying laps.

You'll see, here and now.

• CHAPTER ONE •

Love at
first sight

'I GOT IN at a very early age. I was crazy about all kinds of machines – everything with wheels, two wheels or four wheels or even five wheels! I was really interested and I loved it. When I was about five, my mother was working as well as my father and we couldn't get a nanny or anything so I'd go with my father to where he worked. It was about half an hour from Helsinki and fortunately close to a racing circuit, Keimola. I always heard the noises, you know, engines running *whaam* and cars going round as if Keke Rosberg [World Champion, 1982] was driving them! I heard these noises: cars going round and motor bikes going round and I decided to go there.

'I can't remember exactly whether I went with friends or by myself. I was very small so I wasn't sure if I'd be allowed to go, but I do remember one visit to the circuit when my parents were with me. I saw this kart and it looked great, really exciting. A friend hired the kart and drove round the track and that looked great, too. I loved it! When we got home I said to my parents *this is real fun, we have to go back*, and my parents said *OK, we'll go*. We hired a go-kart. I went out and the very first lap I had a huge shunt. I rolled over, the whole thing – I mean a serious shunt – and my father ran to me. That's my very first memory of the racing.

'No, I wasn't scared at all by the shunt. I saw my father's face and he was very scared. I understood then that it's not nice if that happens, it's not good. So while the shunt did not put me off, it did make me realise the effect motor sport can have on other people. I think I understood from then on that you always try and leave a little margin, you don't drive totally at the edge. Was that a mature attitude for a five-year-old? I suppose so.

'Anyway, after the shunt my parents weren't so keen, but I said to them I **must** get a go-kart. I kept repeating that every day for weeks and eventually they bought me a go-kart, a very small go-kart. I remember the colour – it was blue, a blue go-kart with a black seat. It had a very old engine and it had been Henri Toivonen's [a celebrated rally driver who won the RAC Rally twice and was killed during the 1986 Tour de Corse].

'Anyway, that's how I got started. When I was a kid I used to love driving so much that I cried when my dad told me I had to stop for the day. I loved this sport and my parents started making friends around this go-kart, and other young kids were there who had the same hobby so it was fantastic, the whole atmosphere.'

Mika Hakkinen was born on 28 September 1968 to Harri and Aila. The family lived in an apartment in Vantaa, some ten kilometres north of Helsinki. Harri was, and is, a short-wave radio operator who communicates information to boats in the Gulf of Finland and also handles emergencies. When the children were young, Aila worked as a part-time secretary.

Harri describes the young Mika as 'not the leader-of-the-gang type but, rather, more quiet. He was polite to others, especially older people. He wasn't shy but he would rather listen to what other people said than talk about what he himself had done. He had lots of friends in the building where our apartment was but most were older, only a year or two, but at that stage it makes a difference.'

Aila insists that as a child Mika 'never walked, he was always running around. Some of our friends often asked if he *could* walk! He didn't want to be in one place very long.'

Harri explains that 'near my job was the Keimola racing circuit and that was the place where Mika started his karting. He turned over a kart we had rented at the circuit. That kart was big and higher than they are nowadays. After the accident he jumped up almost immediately and, I recall, he never did have a serious accident.

'Beside my regular job at the radio station I worked as a part-time taxi driver in order to get the money to buy Mika's first kart. I drove taxis for six years – every free day I had – to pay all the increasing

Right It all started here (Hakkinen family).

16

The inventive Hakkinens put this together for youngsters to play on (Hakkinen family).

expenses which this karting started to create. Mika needed petrol, Mika needed tyres and it seemed there were never enough of those. Mika's first kart, which had belonged to Toivonen, we paid 1000 Finnmarks (about £125). Every evening – or night – when I got home after driving the taxi I used to roll up a 10 Finnmark note and put it into a huge bottle which you could not see inside. I did this for a long time and once Aila was cleaning the apartment she found the bottle and discovered all the notes in it. There was a total of more than 1100 Finnmarks and we used that money to buy the Toivonen kart. It was a blue Zip-kart with an American engine.'

Aila was quite content with all this because 'buying a kart for Mika seemed so natural. He liked to drive *so* much. We never even stopped to think it could be dangerous. Moreover it made us do something together, as a family, because clearly Mika couldn't go to the circuits by himself. It took so much of our time and money that not until recently were we able to complete our summer cabin 150 kilometres north of Helsinki' – Harri points out that last summer [1996] 'we were able to complete it properly. We remade the floors and all sorts of things, so that today we can say it is finally finished!' He points out that directing the money to Mika's karting made this take so long but also that 'all our spare time was spent with Mika competing in karting events.'

Scandinavia is a big place and, Harri says, competing involved a great deal of travelling, 'all over Scandinavia and then, when he became better, we also travelled around [mainland] Europe. We always drove, never flew anywhere, not possible – we had to transport the kart as well as ourselves. We had a Volkswagen minibus and that was it.'

Aila described young Mika as a 'kind child who wasn't anything special at school. Sometimes he said that school would be nice if he could just do sport and art and handicrafts. Maths, history and other subjects like that were not that interesting to him. He didn't read much. He was drawn towards *active* things. However, in elementary school (7 or 8 years) he got a prize for being the best pupil in his class – but that meant he was taking part in all his classes, not finishing top of them! When he left school he enrolled on a course to become a metal

Who could have guessed he would later drive a car like this (McLaren).

worker.' (The racing career quickly banished all notions of that, of course.)

And here's a thought. Harri explains that while Mika was at elementary school a teacher explained how you could learn to be a musician *and* learn the skills which circus performers have. Mika liked that and went to a special evening school . . .

I asked Hakkinen to trace the seeds of the early career.

Is there a history of motor racing in the family?

'Yes and no. My mother and my father never did race, but my mother's brother was crazy for cars, crazy, crazy, crazy. The family on my mother's side were interested in all kinds of things like that – not my mother, but all the rest. They were crazy about anything – *anything* – that was helped by an engine: aeroplanes, motor bikes, cars. I tell you, they built amazing things and I loved it. I am sure that a lot of influence on my career came from there. With their hands they were able, particularly my uncle, to build these different things, cars, rallycross cars, rally cars. Uncle was not my mother's real brother but – how do you call it? – stepbrother. He is 15 years older than I am and when I was ten I went every weekend with him to the place where he worked on the cars. We didn't sleep at night, we built the cars until 3 o'clock, 4 o'clock in the morning.'

That was where you fell in love with it?

'I think so.'

Was it you who wanted to race karts?

'Yes, and my father said OK.'

But no doubt your mother said no.

'She didn't say no. My mother loved it because it was a family sport, it brought the family together and it was a challenge. My mother wanted to give me something that I liked, and I liked the karting, so *go for it, my son!* I'd describe my upbringing as more or less middle class. Why I'm saying more or less is that they always spent all the money on the racing. They could have had a nice house or whatever they wanted to have, but they spent the money on the racing, on the karting.'

Why?

'They liked it and they wanted to give something wonderful to their kids so the kids could be happy. Maybe they didn't have that when they were kids.'

What about your sister?

Pedal power. This demon-looking bike, Hakkinen says, was built of pieces from everything and caused deep envy among other kids – although the engine wasn't real! (Hakkinen family).

A fifth birthday party. Hakkinen is sure that's what it is because there's a present on the TV behind him (Hakkinen family).

Six years old with pet Titon (Hakkinen family).

Horse power (Hakkinen family).

'My sister is three years older than I am. She used to do horse-riding. She tried karting but she wasn't that good and didn't like it.'

Karting is a self-contained little world, which, when the youngsters enter it, regularly embraces parents as well, each finding much within it.

There are several important aspects to how Hakkinen describes his way into motor sport: the basic appeal of noise and movement at such a tender age, the use of the word 'love', but to me most significantly the first-lap crash, which might have put him off for life but worked entirely the other way, confirming that this was what he wanted to do.

Bombing round a tight little track on a go-kart can be a hobby, a way of passing the time, and/or just plain exciting. Many youngsters progress quite naturally towards racing, a serious step and one far removed from simply bombing round. Racing invariably has consequences. In Finland you couldn't race until you were 12, and, preparing for that, the Hakkinen family contacted a man called Pekka Pirkola, who had been importing and making karts for years. Pirkola had seen Hakkinen practising and 'although he was too young to race yet, he was extremely fast. They bought a kart from me, my own production Finnkart, and we started together in 1980. His father was a very normal man, he hadn't much money, and that's normal, too (chuckle).' Hakkinen's father had been acting as mechanic, a role Pirkola would now also fill.

'Our first trip to a race was in the north of Finland, at Kemora [one of the three main Finnish circuits] 500 kilometres from Helsinki,' Pirkola says. 'Mika hardly spoke. In fact, I had driven 300 kilometres before he said anything! He didn't speak much because he was very much alone with his thoughts and he only liked driving. He didn't win so much that first year – 1980 – but he did the second year, taking the 85cc class at the Finnish Championships, then the Championships themselves four times, 1983/84/85/86. This was a sensation [because

'I couldn't play the guitar then, and I can't play it now!' (Hakkinen family).

nobody had done it before]. Mika speaks a lot more now than he used to (chuckle).'

I wonder if the fact that young Hakkinen didn't speak much created problems.

'Because he couldn't tell what was happening with the kart, this was a problem. Yes, he liked only driving! If the engine was fast, that was enough! I know that Michael Schumacher was different and would say *this is not good, that is not good, this must be better.* Mika only liked the driving! Even when he was so small, I thought he would be a driver all his life. And in a kart he didn't have to think about the techniques, he could just do it.'

Hakkinen concedes the point about shyness. 'I was shy when I was little, but not on the racetrack, though. Off it yes, very shy.'

He remembers a race in Sweden called the Ronnie Peterson Memorial Cup after the Swedish driver who died following an accident in the 1978 Italian Grand Prix at Monza. 'It was a kart race and there were, like, hundreds of Swedish kids and only one Finn. That was me! I won the race and that was an incredible feeling because Ronnie Peterson's father gave me the trophy. It was not many years after Ronnie's death. Ronnie was a big hero – Ronnie was *the* big hero and people still talk about him as one of the fastest guys of all time. It was a very big day for me, even though I was only a little kid.'

Were you emotional?

'No. I'm not a very emotional guy.'

Hakkinen remembers an early race that he won and 'my father cried. It was a shock, because normally Finns don't do that and at that age you think your parents are so strong, they will never be affected like that by things like that. I realised how much my winning had meant to him. The tears? We never mentioned this again, never discussed it.'

Pirkola says that 'when he was 14, 15 he said that one day he would drive in Formula 1 and he would become World Champion. He said it seriously, not for a joke. Everything was only driving. I said it was possible that what he had said about Formula 1 could come true because I have seen many drivers – myself and Keke Rosberg were driving at the same time in karts – and I think Mika was faster than Keke. And in Finland at any given time there are normally about a thousand good karters and 40 tracks, so it's a big sport and a high standard. To win the Finnish Championship is not easy.'

Age six, and the first go-kart, a McCulloch – 'It might have been an Irish kart!' The chassis had been Henri Toivonen's (Hakkinen family).

Pirkola explains why Hakkinen's thoughts were projected towards Formula 1 and not to becoming a rally driver like virtually every other red-blooded young male in Finland. 'He only liked driving on tracks. Never did he say he'd drive in a rally. I know he tested in a rally car but he didn't like it – always he said he liked this formula of tracks.'

Hakkinen, incidentally, disputes this. He insists that he *loved* rally cars but decided not to go in that direction for the most pragmatic of reasons, which we shall be hearing about soon. The decision, however, did represent a departure from the norm. Because of Finland's northern latitude and its harsh climate – especially the long, darkened winters – the country is natural terrain for producing rally drivers, among them Timo Makinen, Hannu Mikkola, Toivonen, Timo Salonen, Ari Vatanen, Markku Alen and Juha Kankkunen; and there is room to learn the art of rallying. Finland's area is 337,030sq km with a population of five million (compared to, say, Italy, with 301,245sq km and a population of 57 million).

If you dream of podiums, practise being on them. The girl in the yellow jumper is sister Nina (Hakkinen family).

A track called Umea, Sweden, 1978. 'I'll never forget it. There was so much rain that people pretended to fish in the paddock.' (Hakkinen family).

Certainly in the early 1980s Hakkinen was an authentic Finnish champion, and in 1984 he travelled to Laval, France, to contest the World Junior Karting Championship. *Karting magazine* wrote:

'**Heats.** The stars of the first day were Michael Schumacher and Mika Hakkinen, whilst the second day were Yvan Muller and Paul Tracy. Schumacher was the driver to beat in the Junior Worlds last year at Horrem in Germany, since his father runs the track and he spends every afternoon at it. Reliability was his problem last year, and it was going to be interesting whether he had overcome this handicap. One thing that had certainly not changed was his driving style, his peculiar lean and his two-wheeling antics. Hakkinen from Finland, although a relative unknown and going into the meeting on a limited budget, soon caught the eye.

'**Pre-Final.** One thing both Tracy's and Hakkinen's fathers had in common for the pre-Final was that neither of them were going to watch it. The former paced up and down the back of the spectator area asking "How is he doing now?", whilst the latter sat in the pits with butterflies in his stomach.

'At the start Schumacher, from the outside, took the lead followed by Muller. Hakkinen had a very bad start, suffering from carburation problems that had not been cured after carburation practice. The two leaders soon pulled out a small lead, with Hakkinen leading the next group. Hakkinen was slow down the straight and on lap 3 [Antonio] Miani [Italy] went past. Half a lap later Hakkinen was out as [Roberto] Colciago [Italy] tried to get past and they both came off.' Tracy, incidentally, is the current successful IndyCar driver.

Reflecting, Hakkinen says, 'I remember Schumacher in karts. At this stage of their lives, however, most kids don't speak a foreign language so they find it difficult to communicate. You just come and race and go away. That's what happened.'

During the karting years Hakkinen met another Mika – surnamed Sohlberg, whose father Kari was President of the Finnish Automobile Sport Federation and also had a competitive team called *Blue Rose*. 'We met the first time in a small sort of kids' party after a go-kart weekend,' remembers Sohlberg. 'It must have been around 1982 because he started to drive for the *Blue Rose* team that year, Pekka alongside him.

'To compete internationally you need some money – not a lot, but some – and when Mika started we were providing the finance. My father was looking for talented young drivers. We'd already had rally drivers. I was doing go-karts and I became friends with Mika. Through that, Mika joined the *Blue Rose* team, and that's how it really started. All he wanted to do was drive.

'He was very shy, and I can believe the story Pekka tells about Kemora and not speaking. Mika was shy because, really, what he had done since he was six was drive go-karts and be with his family. He hadn't been abroad or things like that, so it was quite normal, especially for the Finnish mentality. Finnish people are very shy, very, very shy people.'

I point out that the ones I've met certainly aren't shy.

'Yes, but the ones you've met are international people who, perhaps, have what you might call international influence. If you go to Finland and speak to the people in the street they are shy, first of all because they don't speak such good English – even though everyone gets quite a good education, or very good compared to the standards of England – but still the Finnish mentality is restricting yourself: you are a bit careful, you're not like [other] Europeans who throw you into a conversation before you know what's happening. I am sure Keke Rosberg was like that to start with, and, if you look at Mika now, he's not a shy person any more, obviously.'

I'm indebted to journalist Martin Holmes for this further – and lovely – insight, which appeared in *Pirelli World Rallying 1996–1997*: 'Those who have worked in the sport for any length of time know there is something different about the Finns. Their difficult language prevents us from understanding them well – and in turn stops them from being able to express themselves to foreigners with precision. Their famous staccato exclamations show the problem. The absence of the expression "please" in their language does not help! These barriers make their breakthrough into the outside world even more worthy. There are many other curious characteristics about Finns. They have a special sixth sense. As they travel the world they sense when they are in proximity with another Finn. But above all, the most curious hallmark is the way they want to help each other in their lives.'

[The *Short Dictionary of Languages* by Teach Yourself Books, London, describes Finnish as 'agglutinative structure; nouns distinguish singular/plural but not gender, 16 "cases" by suffixation, but some of these are dropping out in favour of prepositional constructions, verb

Make the podium out of whatever nature provides. The woman presenting Hakkinen with the trophy is his mum. Why mum? 'Karting is a family sport and it was a nice gesture to ask her to' (Hakkinen family).

Close combat (Hakkinen family).

shows perfect, imperfect, and combined present/future, and a profusion of infinitives and participles.' In simple terms, damned tricky. Its only real relative is Hungarian, another language that is not – let us say – on the tip of everyone's tongue. Incidentally, Rosberg's sister Jatta confirmed that 'please' does not exist and explained that people think Finns rude as a consequence, although they're not. She added that she spent years and years studying Finnish grammar and it still baffles her.]

A lot of youngsters who will go on and become good racing drivers take to karting naturally and straight away, I venture to Sohlberg. Was it the same with Hakkinen?

'Yes, yes, yes! He was by far the best go-kart driver although his international results don't reflect how good he was because during that time Finns didn't get the same equipment as some other countries. When Mika was driving he never got the best engines.'

Evidently the two Mikas indulged in young men's adventures. The British magazine *Motoring News*, interviewing Sohlberg in 1991, wrote:

'Having watched, and been extremely impressed by a young Mika

Hakkinen racing, Sohlberg persuaded a friend to introduce the two, thus starting a close and competitive friendship. Sohlberg was left to prepare his kart [which he had bought from rally exponent Henri Toivonen] himself, while Hakkinen carved a path towards Formula 1. Sohlberg enjoyed limited success before giving it up after a nasty accident at the age of 17.

'Although racing was never regarded as more than a hobby, Sohlberg had become addicted to driving sideways, racing 1.6-litre Beetles against close friends, including Hakkinen. "Every weekend in the winter we had an ice track at our summer place and we went training there," smiles Sohlberg as the memories come flooding back. "They were rallycross ones and we banged them and we rolled them and we had a really good time. We always had a sauna there and we learnt a lot in that time."'

I invited Sohlberg to expand on this. 'Yes, I had a Volkswagen Beetle and Mika had one. The summer place was about 50 kilometres from

Girls can drive, too, and why not? (Hakkinen family).

Helsinki and in winter we had an ice track there. Roll the cars? Well, they were cheap and we were having really good "fights" and it didn't matter if you touched, but I didn't actually roll. Mika did once. He got out laughing. Incidentally, he claims he was faster than me and I claim I was faster than him. Our memories don't agree about this . . .'

At the end of 1985 Hakkinen decided to do one more year of karting, then move into single-seaters, which would be Formula Ford 1600. However, Pirkola explains that while karting is strong in Finland, 'we have problems when our young drivers go into racing cars because there is not so much money for motor sport. This matter of economics is a big problem. We talked a great deal with an Italian kart manufacturer and this factory gave everything for Mika, but he still changed to Formula Ford.'

At the end of 1986 Pirkola 'talked with Mika and he said he was going to change now to single-seaters. I wanted him to stay in karts because it is very important for your [subsequent] career that you win some major title – the European Championship or World Championship. I told him how important I thought it was to him, but he said he felt it wasn't so important.'

Why did you decide to go to 1600?

'Because,' Hakkinen says, 'Finland already had so many champions in rallying, there was no point in going there any more. I loved rallying, but it was better to go into single-seater racing where we had had only one champion – Keke. We needed some more.'

Did you really think like that?

'Yes.'

Tell me about getting into a 1600 car.

'It was the most disappointing feeling to go from karts to this. It was so slow, it was so slow it was terrible. You go into a corner, it was slow, you'd go sideways, you had no power coming out of the corner. The tyres were grooved. *What the hell is this, a road car or what?* In karts we were so professional, we had qualifying tyres, the kart was on two wheels, every corner pressure and very demanding. The 1600 was like . . . nothing. OK, another difference was that it was more expensive, attracted more publicity. You'd go into a room and people would say *ah, you're a driver now.* But karting was serious stuff.'

Harri points out that 'when Mika started to race in Formula Ford 1600 we bought a used bus in order for us to continue our "hobby." We

You can see the increase of sophistication in the karts as the career progressed (Hakkinen family).

paid for it in instalments for years and it was good to have it, but that bus was another reason why we didn't finish our summer cabin for so long. It was the first time we were able, incidentally, to get some small sponsors for Mika. A major stroke of luck was getting the GWS company to support Mika – very much because Kari Sohlberg's son Mika was driving karts, too, at that time and they had become good friends.'

Karting, Aila insists, was 'just fun to all of us and even when Mika went into Formula Ford 1600 I didn't feel anything special in the sense of feeling *this could be dangerous*. I thought of it as a hobby for him and for us. I never thought that one day racing could be his profession. After, however, the first successes in 1600 we knew that the next step would be even bigger cars and we didn't know how much that would cost or whether we would still be able to finance it.'

Sohlberg explains that 'when Mika went into FF1600 I was the team manager. Well not exactly, but we went around together, me, Mika and two mechanics.'

Hakkinen bought a Reynard that another Finn, JJ Lehto, had used the year before and would contest the Finnish and Swedish Championships plus a couple of rounds of the European Championship, and, in late autumn, the famed and fabled Formula Ford Festival at Brands Hatch.

'We had to travel all the time, and one of the races was in Norway,' Sohlberg says. 'Fifteen races in three championships. We had a bus. Mika adapted to cars very well – he didn't find it hard at all. He is a talent. You put him in a rally car and he's quick; you put him into whatever that's got four wheels – or even just *one* wheel! – and he's quick.

'In Sweden, to start with, we were racing against people we had never heard of at circuits we had never seen. That wasn't a problem for Mika. I always remember his first international win was at the Kinnekullering in Sweden, and afterwards the circuit interviewer asked Mika about his race in Swedish. Mika moved his head to indicate that he didn't speak Swedish. The interviewer asked in English and Mika answered *My race was very easy and my tyres are very hot! Thank you*. When we went to Sweden in the bus, we'd put it on the boat and sleep on the bus. The atmosphere was very happy, very nice. We were like a big family. Mika had already learned a lot from go-karting and he wasn't so shy any more. He started to change very rapidly because he is a bright guy.'

Years later, when he had reached Formula 1, Hakkinen would say, 'The travelling is no problem. I travelled a lot when I was younger, doing go-karting. We used to travel four days in a car. When I was young I was always sleeping in the vans. Now I sleep in hotels. I've been away from home since I was 18 and I don't get homesick or anything like this. It's normal life.'

Hakkinen duly won the Finnish and Swedish and was beating Lehto's times of the year before by up to a second a lap. Someone described him as a 'revelation', and *Autosport* magazine suggested that he was perhaps the 'fastest of all' FF1600 drivers in Europe, which, in context, stood as a considerable accolade.

In the European Championship at Zandvoort he took pole but crashed in the rain; at Zolder in the next round he won. *Autosport*,

The World Junior Championships in Laval, France, 1984. Hakkinen prepares to dominate the first day (Hakkinen family).

under a headline 'Quicker Mika', reported that the name everyone was talking about was 'that of Finn Mika Hakkinen. At Zandvoort Mika had been on pole by 1s. In Belgium he was not so lucky, colliding with another car on his sixth qualifying lap. However, he had already been fleet enough for fifth grid slot.'

In the race a driver called Patrick Dewulf led while 'Hakkinen progressed rapidly past Belgian Karl Frahm and pressured Svend Hansen [for second place]. Frahm tried to fight back at the Finn, but left the road on the exit of the fast left-hander after the pits. The shape of the race changed on lap 8 [of 12], though, when the leader spun out on the back section and Hansen took over with Hakkinen's Reynard in his wake. And the Finn proved why he is so highly rated by moving to the fore on the last lap, using the kerbs and more as he left the first chicane. Dewulf charged, but just failed to regain second.'

That wasn't the end of the season. Two occasions remained, and one of them would open the way to the rest of his life.

CHAPTER TWO

Riding
the Dragon

DONINGTON PARK IN October 1987 was about the future. Major motor sport sponsors Marlboro had organised what you might call 'examinations' as part of their Ladder of Opportunity scheme. Under the gaze of a judging panel which included Ron Dennis (McLaren), former World Champion James Hunt and Hughes de Chaunac (French ORECA team), a carefully sifted sample of up-and-coming drivers showed what they could do. If they 'passed' they were to receive full sponsorship for the following season, something of enormous value early in a career.

'I was really nervous before Donington,' Hakkinen says, 'but not because of the driving. I was nervous because of the people, English-speaking people, big team managers, sponsors. James Hunt was there and Hughes de Chaunac, etc. So I was nervous about the people. I saw Marlboro colours, big trucks, all very professional and I thought *My God*, you know, but I knew I could do the driving.

'I mean, there were German drivers in these trials, English drivers and so on, but I said to myself *we've come from Finland and we know how to do it*. Already psychologically I felt strong when I got there. *We're from the karting and the snow and ice, we already have our rally champions* [and Rosberg!], *we aren't afraid of anybody.* So I came and I did it.'

At the end, the recipients were Jean Alesi and Volker Weidler (being promoted by Rosberg, incidentally), who secured seats in Formula 3000; Eddie Irvine and JJ Lehto, who secured seats in Formula 3; and 'two young drivers' – Allan McNish and Hakkinen – who secured seats in the newly announced Vauxhall Lotus Challenge. They'd drive for a team called Dragon.

Autosport reported that 'the selection was based on a three-day testing session driving a Reynard 87SF FF2000 chassis. The young Scot, still only 17, has shown the benefits of a karting pedigree and impressed greatly in his first year of Formula 1600. The star of the tests, though, was young Finn Hakkinen. His raw pace thoroughly impressed the panel, and FF1600 titles from his Scandinavian exploits prove his worth.' Under a headline 'Hakkinen astounding as Marlboro men graduate', the magazine added: 'Demonstrating tremendous aggression, he produced no fewer than eight laps in the 1m 11s bracket, leaving his mark at 1m 11.42s.'

Erkki Mustakari was there. 'I came to know Mika when he participated in the test session at Donington. In fact, that was the first time I met him. There was a great interest in Finland that somebody Finnish was invited to a session like that. There was a real possibility that something good might come out of it. In those days I was a part-time journalist, so I thought this might be good – anyway, JJ Lehto was already racing in England in Formula Ford 2000 and Mika had a genuine chance to do the same thing. However, it always required so much money and if Marlboro invited somebody and afterwards said OK, that would give you a career.

When the engine started and he accelerated you thought Jesus, this is something else

---

'I had heard a little bit of this and a little bit of that about him, and there he was, you know, tall guy, blond hair – a little bit long, that hair in fact, especially at the back of his head. In my eyes he didn't look like a rock-hard racing driver. He looked very average but tall for his age, a blond young man from Finland. He could just as easily have been an ice hockey player or long-distance runner, the way he looked. He did impress me because when I asked him how he had got to Donington he replied *well, I've been driving that big bus*. He was actually driving a bus through England – he did the driving himself, he had the licence to do it – and in that bus he had his own Formula Ford 1600 car! He was preparing for the Formula Ford Festival at Brands Hatch.

'We spent the morning at Donington getting to know each other because it was damp and rainy and the Marlboro people who were running the test wanted to wait until the track got dry. Mika struck me as very shy, I would say so, yes. He'd rather stay quiet than talk, he'd rather listen than talk, but the moment he got in the car you knew exactly that he had a talent. When the engine started and he accelerated you thought *Jesus, this is something else.*

'An interesting little detail on that first meeting was the fact that, when I asked him how long he had been in England, he said close to a week. I said *OK, where have you been staying?* He replied *well, I've been living in this bus.* I said *oh, that must be a really good bus,* and he replied *no, it's a place to have the car. There's enough space to sleep and a little table where I can sit with my mechanic.* It wasn't a McLaren motorhome, you know . . .

'I said *when this test is over we go to my hotel* – I was staying at the Thistle Hotel not far from Donington circuit – *and go to my room and you take a good shower or bath because you need that.* He looked that way. I asked him *have you taken a shower lately?*, and he replied *well . . .*

The decisive day at Donington for Hakkinen and many others including – can you spot them? – McNish, Mark Blundell, Gianni Morbidelli, Eddie Irvine, Roland Ratzenberger, Jean Alesi and Martin Donnelly. Incidentally the man standing three to the right of Hakkinen – as we look at it – is Dick Bennetts (Erkki Mustakari, Finnpremio Oy/Ltd).

'So I took him to my hotel room, he took a shower, and when he came out he said *this feels like being in heaven.* Then I said *and now it's time for me to buy you a decent dinner instead of you spending your time in the fast food places.* So we went down to the restaurant and had a good meal and he felt superb after that. What a day! First of all the test went well, and now this cleaning up business and eating up business. He said this has been a great day and in its own way that has made us really firm friends ever since. He understood that I wanted to do things for him that was more than normal journalism, which I did because I have kids of my own about Mika's age, so I knew he would love that – at least I would have! And he did.'

Aila says that 'after Donington everything changed so much. He had to move to England and so he didn't live with us any more. That was a big change for us. And that was, too, the first time that I thought it could be dangerous.'

A week after Donington Hakkinen was at Brands for the Festival. This year it contained such drivers as fellow Finn Mika Salo – who had raced Hakkinen in karts – Irvine, Alain Menu, Pedro Chaves, Karl Wendlinger and McNish. *Autosport*, previewing the meeting, wrote that 'the Reynard bid does not rest firmly on the shoulders of Menu, because one will also be driven by Formula Ford's latest sensation Mika "Haka" Hakkinen. Hailing from Finland, this 18-year-old has been driving an old Reynard with good effect, carving lumps off his old lap records. Providing he can learn how to cope with the competitiveness of British FF1600 around such a tight track as Brands Hatch, and doesn't have an accident, Mika might well spring the ultimate surprise.'

In his heat he finished third. 'Having forsaken his ex-JJ Lehto Reynard 86FF for a new model, highly touted Mika Hakkinen shared the front row on his first visit to Brands, ahead of the Synchronised Systems RF87 of double Junior Champion Derek Higgins.' The track was still wet, he reached the first corner, Paddock, in third, and stayed there.

In his quarter-final he was 'usurped' by a driver called Mark Poole 'scything' by at Paddock, and 'on the final lap Derek Daly [not the former Formula 1 driver of course] jumped on a mistake by the Finn and nipped through for fifth.'

Hakkinen, then, was sixth. In his semi-final he and a driver called Neil

Cunningham collided on the way down from the Druids horseshoe. Cunningham had to be cut from his car and was 'removed to the medical centre from where he was later described as "shaken but not stirred".'

Irvine won the final from Menu, McNish fifth. McNish remembers that Hakkinen 'ran pretty well at the Festival until he crashed. However, I also remember his performance was a little bit inconsistent. He ended up in the barrier – mind you, like about 85 per cent of the other drivers at the Festival did . . .'

Reflecting, Hakkinen would explain that for the Festival he had changed cars and 'it was a catastrophe. I couldn't make the car handle at all. I had spent time doing the Marlboro tests instead of testing the Reynard before the Festival.'

The following season, 1988, he prepared to move upwards. The series would be called Formula Vauxhall-Lotus in Britain and Opel-Lotus in Europe, with ten rounds in each Championship. It attracted immediate and huge interest: 1,350 enquiries about competing came from Britain alone. The idea was to produce racing cars in which the young drivers could demonstrate their skill and be directly compared with the drivers around them. The chassis and engines were all identical, and the possibilities of setting the cars up kept to a minimum. The driver could express himself rather than the car expressing him.

Dragon was a new team formed by two men familiar with the ways of motor sport, Hughie Absalom and Doug Bebb. 'We tendered to Marlboro for a budget to do Formula Vauxhall,' Absalom says, 'and we got their backing. They had already done the tests at Donington on who they wanted to drive and they'd picked McNish and Hakkinen. They said *we have the two drivers, here is a budget*, and we were very happy with that.'

Mustakari accompanied Hakkinen to England. 'Kari Sohlberg was Mika's sort of godfather, looking after him because Mika's parents didn't have the financial possibilities to do that. Kari said to me *would you go to England with Mika just in case something comes up that he doesn't understand?* I said I'd love to go. I started around that time taking care of his press service, if I can put it like that. That was part of what Sohlberg wanted me to do.'

'The team,' McNish says, 'had a lot of experience in various forms of motor racing. Hughie had been in Formula 1 [with Leyton House] and other things, and Douglas had been with Williams, so it wasn't just two

Action in the Vauxhall-Lotus, 1988 (Zooom, courtesy Vauxhall).

guys who decided they wanted to run a motor racing team. The fact that they managed to pick up the Marlboro sponsorship and two drivers they thought would do a reasonable job proved that.'

'I didn't know Mika at all,' Absalom says. 'He was a young kid who could hardly speak any English. He turned up and we got along pretty well, although for the next two and a half, three months it was a matter of working to a piece of paper. That was to translate certain words from Finnish into English and vice versa. It is how we did our conversing. He really could not speak English. For the first couple of test sessions he had a Finnish reporter with him [Mustakari] and the reporter helped in translation.'

I wondered if it was a problem when, say, Mika came into the pits. 'Well, it's like all these things, isn't it? You figure them out somehow or other. We had lots of terminology written on the pieces of paper.'

Mustakari remembers vividly that when Hakkinen 'had to go to London to meet the Dragon Motorsport people, Kari Sohlberg asked

Car control in the Vauxhall-Lotus (Zooom, courtesy Vauxhall).

me if I could go along to help him in case of any language difficulties. That was OK with me. When we were taking our seats in the plane Mika asked if he could sit by the window. I said *yes, sure*. Then I asked him how often he'd flown before. *Once, when I was a little kid!* he said. So here was a young driver who was to become a real professional and

he was in an aeroplane for only the second time in his life in 1988 – less than ten years ago!'

Mustakari says, 'The thing is that people who don't understand a language keep on saying *yeah* to everything because they feel that they don't want to look stupid, but in fact saying *yeah* to everything makes them look stupid. I always said to Mika *if you don't understand don't say "yes", say "I don't understand"*. Then people know that you are thinking yourself. You can't say yes to everything, and if the car that you drive feels good or feels bad – well, if it feels good say that, if it feels bad say that also – because that is exactly what they want to know. Sometimes they even make mistakes on purpose because they want to see if this guy notices, especially in testing situations.'

Dragon found Hakkinen somewhere to live, but, because the first race wasn't until early April, he returned to Finland and his National Service. 'I think he went back for about three weeks because we had a lull in the action and he had to go and do some of his National Service . . . and an intensive course in English. He was in the army and he had to go back every so often. I suppose it was a bit like our TA.'

The commentator was livid: This Finn was beating the Scots on their home ground

---

It wasn't like our Territorial Army at all. 'There was a special battalion for sports people,' Hakkinen says. 'That means people who already had a serious career in sport. That didn't mean they were exempt from anything, no! We had to learn to shoot guns and all the rest of it. I learned a lot about comradeship and being part of a team and I've never forgotten. You try marching 20, 30 kilometres into the forest when it's really, really cold – like it gets in Finland in winter – and then you have to put up the tents. You are so tired that all you want to do is lie down and sleep. That's when people act as a team, relying on each other, doing it together, helping each other. It's something that is also very valid in a motor sport team, and I have always been able to relate to it.'

To McNish, Hakkinen was almost a complete stranger. McNish is sure he hadn't raced against him in karting 'because he was older than I was and consequently when I raced in the juniors he'd have been a senior. I only did one season of European karting at senior level, but there were two classes at that point, the 135cc and the 100cc – he was racing the 135, I was racing the 100 – so I didn't really know him until we arrived together at the Marlboro evaluation test at Donington, and then the Formula Ford Festival a week later.'

The impression Hakkinen made on him at Donington was 'basically a fast driver with a lot of natural ability. Don't forget it was an evaluation test and effectively we were all trying to land the same job [Marlboro backing], and for that reason we didn't speak very much. I wouldn't say that any of the drivers socialised. My Finnish was certainly not very good and his English wasn't very good, which meant we couldn't speak much anyway, but obviously you take note of what is happening around you, and when Mika was out in the car he was quick, taking it to the edge *as usual*.'

I propose to examine the season's races – and the races of the following two seasons – in some detail to capture the gathering momentum of Hakkinen's career, including the problems and setbacks. I also give what McNish did because, as ever, the most valid measurement of a driver is how he compares to his team-mate.

Thruxton. Hakkinen pole from a Belgian, Philippe Adams, McNish third. In the race McNish got on to the power fastest and went round Hakkinen, Adams leading. Hakkinen ran fifth, recovered and at the start of lap 10 of the 15 found a way past Adams – which McNish had already done. Hakkinen closed on McNish, setting fastest lap, but his clutch was failing and he accepted second place, prudently slowing over the final two laps.

Silverstone. Adams pole from Hakkinen, McNish (hampered by an electrical fault) 12th. In the race Adams made a better start, Hakkinen harrying him for three laps before taking him and spending the next six laps building a winning cushion.

'I got to know Mika relatively quickly,' McNish says, 'because he moved across to the UK and we did a tremendous amount of testing at the beginning. With racing in the two championships through the season we were effectively on the road together for quite long periods of time. We were living in the same house, and to be honest I found him very easy to get on with. The fact that we were successful helped the situation, in as much as the team were quite happy: if one of us didn't win, the other one generally did. Mika was obviously fast, but that was, I feel, a good thing from my point of view because it pushed me. I was intent on beating everyone else, but very intent on beating him.'

Donington. McNish pole, Hakkinen fourth. They led into Redgate and drew away from the field, but reached oil dropped by another driver at the entry to the chicane. They both saw the red and yellow warning flag, but the extent of the 'slick' almost deceived them – McNish nearly slithered. Towards the end, Hakkinen forced McNish to make a couple of mistakes, but his oil temperature was rising and he backed off, ran to the end second again.

Mallory Park. A Briton, Peter Hardman, pole from Hakkinen, but McNish was punished because the car's rear ride height was illegally low – he started from the back and with a 10-second penalty. The race needed a re-start after a crash and Hardman led from Hakkinen while McNish worked his way up. Hakkinen set fastest lap, making a late, dogged attempt on Hardman, who had a brake balance problem that might have left him vulnerable at the hairpin. Hardman resisted and won by 0.3 of a second, McNish fifth.

Knockhill. Hakkinen qualified third, McNish fourth. *Autosport*, reporting the race, said that 'at the front Hakkinen fell back from Andy Sim [a Brit] and looked to be in trouble. "I didn't know what it was,' said Mika, 'but after a while the car came good, as if the engine had been off for a while." His sudden resurgence brought him under the rear wing of Sim's car, McNish now some 4 seconds in arrears but pulling away from Gary Ayles. By lap 15 [of 25] things were hotting up at the sharp end of the race, Hakkinen trying his hardest to pass Sim, diving down the outside into the hairpin, looking to be on the ragged edge. Coming out of the hairpin, however, the Finn had better traction and he pulled alongside Sim before taking the lead.

'By now it all looked to be over because, in the course of the next three laps, McNish caught and passed Sims as well, their short battle allowing the championship leader to open up a comfortable lead. The commentator was livid: this Finn "Miko Heineken" was beating the Scots on their home ground. Unfortunately for Mika, he soon reached parts no others could when his throttle stuck open at the start of lap 22, the Marlboro car diving off the left-hand side of the circuit, bouncing across the track and finishing up in the long grass. The mechanics verified the jammed throttle, but Mika remained philosophical. "It was going well up until then, wasn't it?"' McNish won, giving him 68 points, Hakkinen 65, Ayles 40.

Thruxton. McNish pole, Hakkinen third. Hardman won, McNish third, Hakkinen fourth, decided on the aggregate of two races because the first was halted after a crash – again.

The European Championship began at Zandvoort, and *Autosport*, reporting the qualifying, said that 'Hakkinen stole pole by 0.02 sec in the final period. The day started badly for Mika, his Dragon Motorsport

The team of 1988, starring Hakkinen and, next to him, Allan McNish (Zooom, courtesy Vauxhall).

Marlboro entry suffering a clutch failure so he was unable to complete more than two laps and languished 35th overall as a result. Cool as you like, however, the 19-year-old went out in the second session and rocketed through to pole. He was precise and determined – and it showed.' McNish qualified eighth.

In the race, Hakkinen emerged from the horseshoe Tarzan corner at the end of the start-finish straight with a clear lead from Dane Henrik Larsen, but by lap 15 of the 20 seemed in trouble because Larsen had drawn full up to him.

'I suddenly found the car starting to understeer,' Hakkinen said, 'and I lost a lot of time. Maybe the front wing dropped a bit and I lost downforce. I don't know, but I adjusted it and it was OK to the end.' McNish, beset by mechanical problems, came 10th.

The season intensified.

Donington. This seventh round of the British Championship was a week after Zandvoort, Hakkinen pole from McNish. Hakkinen led the race throughout but was penalised a minute for creeping the start, relegating him to 12th. McNish 100 points, Hakkinen 75, Ayles 54.

The second European round, at Paul Ricard, was a support to the French Grand Prix, Hakkinen fastest in both practice sessions. He won the race easily enough from Dutchman Peter Kox. McNish dropped out at quarter distance when the battery failed.

We have reached approximately mid-season and, as I've said, the most accurate measure of any driver is how he fares against his team-mate. Frequently, and sometimes inevitably, their co-existence brings friction. I asked McNish to explore this.

'The fact that we were both fighting for the Championships did put on a little bit of a strain at certain times, but nothing that we didn't get over. We didn't have a situation where we didn't speak to each other or anything like that, no question of such a thing at all. In fact, overall, I judge I got on with Mika better than any other team-mate I've had.'

You were into a long examination of two young men, weren't you?

'Well, it was and, yes, we were young, but you have to remember as well that we were out there doing our best; we were enjoying what we were doing, and really we were just at the start of what we were both hoping would be long careers in the sport. Therefore I don't think we were fully aware of all the things that can come creeping in and all the pressures that can bring themselves to bear. Certainly the pressures weren't there to the same extent that they are now for younger drivers. We weren't under the spotlight except that people expected us to work hard to do well. We were under pressure from that. Mika's English had started to get better relatively quickly because he was living here and having to speak English to anyone who was around.'

McNish and Hakkinen shared a house near the Dragon team's headquarters at Newbury, Berkshire. At the time McNish said: 'We don't swop driving secrets but we have developed the ability to switch off, and the result is an excellent working relationship and a friendship.' Despite this, McNish felt from the start of the season that Hakkinen would be 'my chief opposition. My winning the first race was an important psychological victory. Thruxton did give me an advantage and my year seemed to snowball after that.'

Hakkinen describes staying in the same house as 'fantastic, we had a good time. We had fun, we had fun together. I wasn't really living in the house because I was going out a lot! Everything was very new for me, coming to England, racing for a team, driving with a Scottish driver. My English wasn't perfect and his English wasn't perfect either! It was interesting and challenging.

'We competed fairly always. Allan and I didn't have problems. I think we had excellent, healthy competition on the track, sometimes really hard, wheel-to-wheel, you know. I won the European Championship and he won the British – that was good, but all the time I wanted to win both. In the British I had really bad luck. My throttle got stuck in the Knockhill race when I was leading by half a lap. We were due to race in Birmingham [as a support for the round of the European F3000], but it was cancelled because of an accident in the 3000. It got dark and we couldn't go out, so another race lost. I learned a lot from Allan. He was very professional that year compared to me; he took everything so seriously that it was unbelievable for me. He was only 18, 19 years old. It was good for me to watch this because I said

Below and following Absolute domination in the second round of the Opel-Lotus Euroseries at the Paul Ricard circuit: pole, fastest lap, victory.

On the podium are (right) Dutchman Peter Kox, second, and Dane Henrik Larsen, third (Zooom, courtesy Vauxhall).

hold on a second, concentrate on driving not business, you're only a kid. Race. That's what I did. I raced.'

McNish today reflects that 'in the races I don't think we crashed. If anything could have been seen as tension, it was diluted by the fact that generally we were both up at the front, and if one didn't win, the other did. That helped.'

Absalom remembers it a little harder. 'Two leading drivers bringing problems? We had that in that first year, we had problems – well, they could have become serious problems where they were actually fighting each other on the track. I had to sit them down one day and say *the only two people who can sort this thing out are you two*, and they did. There'd been a couple of times when they'd almost taken each other off. The way I said it was *if you two guys don't sort it out I'll sort it out for you.* If that had happened, they would have had to drive to whatever we wanted them to – we didn't have team orders.'

This was a powerful threat because a team holds the right to determine which order its drivers run in. This right has been known to baffle outsiders to motor sport, particularly when a pit board is held out ordering one driver to allow the other to overtake. The power of Absalom's threat was that both drivers had very real chances of both championships, but the team might decide who got what – and maybe who didn't get anything. However, Absalom explains that 'we had an ideal situation shaping up where Mika could win the European and Allan win the British. It did cross my mind a couple of times that that would be perfect, but it was turning out that way anyway. We didn't try and arrange it, we just let it happen.'

Was Hakkinen subject to wild moments?

'You learn about a driver as you go along,' Absalom says. 'I mean, when he turned up, to us he was blindingly quick, and when you are up front and getting the job done how can you say he's wild? I think myself that the wild bit came later, when we did Formula 3 – when it was a lot of hard work, you know.'

And a question to McNish: *Was it tough to drive against him?*

'When one of us got in front, it is pretty fair to say it was very, very hard for the other to overtake,' McNish says. 'I can't remember off the top of my head where one of us was ahead and got overtaken by the other. The cars were very evenly matched and the people were all fishing in the dark to try and find the best set-up because it was the first year of the championship.

'Mika had a different driving style to mine. My style was smooth. I'd come out of karting and Formula Ford and, to be honest, I didn't really get on with Formula Ford as well as I'd have liked. I didn't feel I had very much grip. You jumped into a Vauxhall Lotus, it was like heaven in comparison. So my style was smooth – you always kept her in line – whereas Mika just drove on the ragged edge all the time, and if it wasn't on the circuit it would be on the kerbs, and if it wasn't on the kerbs it would be kissing the grass beyond them. That is the way he got time out of that car, and I think he managed to get a lot of time out of the car by doing it that way whereas I did it another way. Consequently our set-ups were slightly different. He needed a lot more out of the rear of the car than I did, and I needed a lot more out of the front than he did. That is something that he may have had to change when he reached Formula 3, whereas, with my style, I was able to get on with Formula 3 a little bit easier.'

The third round of the Euroseries, at Silverstone, was another Grand Prix support race (and co-incidentally also round eight of the British Championship). McNish qualified second but Hakkinen 11th, and both complained of handling difficulties. In the race, on a wet, dank, overcast day, McNish battled to second behind Larsen, Hakkinen eighth. British Championship: McNish 120 points, Hakkinen 87, Ayles 54. European: Larsen 47, Hakkinen 43, Kox 35, McNish joint fifth on 16.

At Hockenheim – round four of the European – Kox took pole from Hakkinen, McNish fourth. In a wet race Hakkinen made a strong start, leading from Kox and Larsen – but Larsen stole past both of them, Hakkinen reportedly 'wavering' on the damp patches at the chicanes. He finished fourth, directly in front of McNish. Larsen 67, Hakkinen 56, Kox 35, McNish still fifth, 23.

I had traction problems, and it was incredible how Mika could put the power down so much better

---

Hakkinen struck back at Spa a week later. Although he only qualified sixth (McNish third), *Autosport* reported that 'after the first qualifying session Hakkinen had provisional pole. This didn't come to anything, though, as he left the track at Pouhon [a left-hander out at the back of the circuit] in the second session after a reputed incident with team-mate Allan McNish. This was no more than a paddock rumour, though . . .'

A German, Marco Werner, took pole in this second session, but that made no difference: Kox led and built the lead to a couple of seconds, Hakkinen closing very slightly, but they came upon a safety vehicle making its way to a crash at the Bus Stop, the artificial semi-chicane near the pits. This enabled Hakkinen to close further, and by the next lap an ambulance had arrived. The race wasn't stopped and the presence of the ambulance enabled Hakkinen to draw up to Kox, slipstreaming him and 'sneaking' past on the outside on lap 8 of the 10. McNish finished third, giving Hakkinen 77, Larsen 67, Kox 50, McNish 37.

At Knutstorp, Sweden, a week later, Kox took pole from Hakkinen (McNish sixth), but at the start of the race Hakkinen stormed away from him. 'I had traction problems,' Kox said, 'and it was incredible how Mika could put the power down so much better.' Hakkinen moved further and further away, McNish coming in third. Hakkinen 97, Larsen 67, Knox 65, McNish 49.

At Brands – round seven of the European – McNish took a mighty pole (Hakkinen third) and, in the race, could not be caught however much pressure Hakkinen placed upon him. When it was over Hakkinen seemed pleased enough with second because it made him all but unbeatable in the Championship with 113 points, Larsen 79, McNish 69 and only the Nurburgring, Estoril and Jerez remained.

Motor racing is rarely straightforward, however.

At the Nurburgring, a certain Heinz-Harald Frentzen took pole, Hakkinen ninth as he struggled to come to terms with the circuit. The race began in drizzle but Hakkinen risked slick tyres. He gained places when cars in front spun off, but, with two laps remaining, spun himself and rammed the tyre wall at the corner before the pits. He pressed on with his nosecone out of joint to finish 12th. Hakkinen 113, Larsen 100, McNish 77.

The British Championship now resumed at, ironically, the Irish circuit of Mondello Park, Hakkinen taking pole and the race no trouble, flag-to-flag, with McNish a delighted second – enough for the Championship, which was, he said immediately afterwards, 'all we set out to achieve and now we're there. It's a great feeling.' McNish 135, Hakkinen 107.

How did Hakkinen take being beaten by his team-mate? 'I can't remember exactly now,' McNish says, 'but I think in pretty good spirits. I certainly took it in pretty good spirits! [McNish's father Bert applied this literally, having taken a bottle of Scotch to celebrate.] We were both on the front row and Mika got the jump on me into the first corner and I sat behind and finished second. I only needed to be fifth for the Championship.'

At Estoril, Frentzen took pole and won from Larsen, Hakkinen qualifying fourth and finishing 13th. He was contesting second place with Larsen when, on lap 15 of the 19, he tried to overtake on the run up the hill out of the first hairpin. Larsen cut across and they collided, the back of Larsen's car damaging Hakkinen's nosecone.

The sort of photograph you'll treasure for ever. Hakkinen and McNish meet Ayrton Senna. Eddie Irvine looks pretty happy too (Zooom, courtesy Vauxhall).

Hakkinen was reported to be 'furious'. Larsen 115, Hakkinen 113, McNish 77.

At Jerez Hakkinen qualified third and finished third, Larsen fourth; but thereby hangs a tale, because on lap 6 of the 17 McNish thrust up the inside of Larsen on the long straight. That prevented Larsen from launching an attack on Hakkinen, but ironically McNish, who finished fourth, was disqualified.

'I think Mika would have been very disappointed if he hadn't beaten Larsen for the Championship after he hadn't managed to win the British,' McNish says. 'At Jerez my tyres were Bridgestone and they had markings on them. You were allowed six tyres for the weekend and had to say on the scrutineering form at the beginning of the weekend which tyres you would be using. The form had been incorrectly filled in, so, as far as the scrutineers were concerned, I had used a tyre that wasn't on the form. I couldn't have won the European Championship by then and, of course, my object was to get as high as I could in the race – but

Mika really needed to beat Larsen. I finished ahead of Larsen, which guaranteed Mika the title, anyway . . .'

. . . or would have done if McNish hadn't been disqualified. Not that it mattered. Hakkinen 126, Larsen 125, McNish 77.

'Larsen was quite a surprise that year,' McNish says, 'because nobody had really heard of him before and he was a wee bit older than we were. He had a good spell in mid-season and then dropped off towards the end. He was running on a very small budget, but he was impressive. Frentzen was in there, David Brabham was in there – a lot of good guys in both championships, actually. If you look solely at the results, fair enough Dragon dominated but it certainly wasn't easy. We didn't go off and win every race at will – we needed to work hard for everything we had.'

Absalom judges that the main thing Hakkinen learned from the season was 'how to cope with big-time motor racing. In hindsight it was little-time racing, but that's not the point if you're involved in it. He learned how to present himself, you know, the usual stuff that young drivers are lacking in. That part of it he learned.'

Also how to win races?

'Well, yes, I suppose that's true, but I don't think races of 30 laps or 30 minutes are quite so taxing. If you are running up front, you should be able to handle it, and he could handle it.'

When you got to know him, what did you make of him as a man?

'You mean a boy! (Laughter) He had a typically Scandinavian-Finnish look, I suppose, but young looking. We tried to treat him and treat Allan McNish as racing drivers rather than kids. You had to make them grow up. You look at yourself and how you were at the same age and you wonder about things like that. One of the best guys we had around helping was James Hunt [who did advisory work for Marlboro]. Hunt was good for both of them because he'd regularly come down, find out how everything was going and give them little pointers. He was very good at that, oh yes. He spent a lot of time doing that; probably spent more time with us than he did with Eddie Irvine and those other guys' – also Marlboro drivers, remember, and further up the ladder.

The final round of the British Championship was at Thruxton on 16 October, and Hakkinen took pole from Larsen. *Autosport* caught the mood of qualifying nicely: 'It was widely expected that Mika Hakkinen would claim pole and so he did, coming out for a typically small number of laps in which he slotted a blinder, the only driver to dip into the 13s. The Finn's nonchalant best was 1m 13.82s, one third of a second better than the best any other could manage.' In the race Hakkinen drove away from Larsen, 'putting on a masterful display of precise driving. No other stood a chance as he obliterated the lap record.' McNish finished third.

Reflecting on the season, Hakkinen said: 'I found that running a car on wings and slicks felt very fast after FF1600, but anyone who has raced karts can adapt. I have enjoyed the racing. I like the way the series has been organised – the way it makes everyone good friends. I'm happy with the way I've driven. Sure, I've made a few mistakes such as putting the car on springs that were too stiff at the Nurburgring and sliding everywhere, not getting any points. Also I was wrong to let myself have an accident with Henrik Larsen at Estoril. It was stupid, but I will learn from it. For next year, though, I will do Formula 3. Many people said I should do Formula 3000, but I'm only just 20 and I don't feel I want to go into 3000 until I am ready. I want to learn to set up a Formula 3 car first.'

Moving from Vauxhall-Lotus to F3 is like going from a sponge pudding to a skateboard

---

Hakkinen tested a Formula 3 car for the first time at Snetteron. It was a Reynard belonging to a team called Pacific Racing, and the man running that team, Keith Wiggins, said: 'He completed around 30 laps in damp but drying conditions and he looked good, doing everything right. Going from Vauxhall-Lotus to F3 is a bit like going from a sponge pudding to a skateboard, and there were obviously one or two facets of his style that he will have to adapt. He was impressive, though, recording successive 62.0-second laps on his final three when the track had almost dried.'

Hakkinen remembers the test vividly 'because I had a bad day. I can evaluate it like that because I had a spin and went off. The Formula 3 car was so low to the ground that I couldn't believe it. In the Lotus you were over the kerbs and everything, then in the Formula 3 car I went off because it touched the ground, slid wide and went on to the gravel. I was annoyed with myself, angry with myself. It was an important test, a really important test, and I went off. I felt like I had failed. I don't remember what Wiggins said, although of course he was unhappy, first time in a Formula 3 car, and maybe he thought I was going much too fast. I went for it. He must have known I was going to do that! I am sure he understood that I was a driver and I wanted to show that I could do laps. The test has always left a bad taste [Hakkinen is speaking about himself, no blame to Wiggins whatsoever]. It didn't work out because your very first test, new formula, new car, what you *don't* do is go off. To be 1 second off the pace is OK, but I repeat, don't go off. I had a bad day and it was not professional to have a bad day like that.'

At season's end, a strange, or perhaps logical, thing happened. For the following season McNish would leave Dragon to join a highly successful Formula 3 team (the next stage upwards). It was called West Surrey Racing, run by a man called Dick Bennetts who had helped Ayrton Senna to the Championship in 1983. Hakkinen, however, stayed with Dragon. McNish explains that 'it had now come to decision time. Mika got on very well with Dragon, they wanted to go up into Formula 3, and Marlboro were willing to support that. Marlboro were supporting West Surrey in Formula 3 as well, and I liked the look of what was happening at West Surrey. I think we were sort of steered in the two directions, if I remember correctly. I don't think there was a situation where it was "you will go here" or "you will go there" or "where would you like to go?" It just fell into place. That's the way it happened. Both of us were comfortable with the way it worked out.'

It happens, however, that the choice you made was right and the choice he made was wrong?

'I must be honest and say that is unfair – unfair to simply say I was right and he was wrong.'

Absalom reflects on Dragon's vulnerability: 'I guess we got slaughtered by various people who thought we had taken on too much in going up to Formula 3. Who slaughtered us? Several of the motoring magazines and probably Mika himself a little bit towards the end of the season because he was so disappointed.'

It is time to explore the delicate matter of equipment, meaning

Right *A deceptive study of Donington in June 1988. McNish (No 9) seems to be leading – but Hakkinen has already gone past the photographer!* (Zooom, courtesy Vauxhall).

which make of car to have and which make of engine to put in it: delicate, because if you get this wrong you are in trouble and because you can't always choose what you'd like to have. Virtually no other sport is like this; to some people it makes motor racing endlessly fascinating, to others completely unsatisfactory because it violates a basic sporting creed: everyone should start with the same chance. Never mind. It is the way it is.

'The story was that we had a choice of buying a Ralt or a Reynard and the engine choice we had was Volkswagen or Toyota,' Absalom says. 'We went the Reynard route because they gave us a good deal and a spare car, which nobody else had in Formula 3 in those days; and we went the Toyota route because the year before JJ [Lehto] had run the same combination and it seemed like the most logical thing to keep everyone happy. We couldn't get a Volkswagen-Spiess *works* deal, anyway, and we couldn't get a Mugen engine, so we took what appeared to be the best route: Toyota. It shouldn't have been a bad decision. The Reynard was probably not as competitive as the Ralt, and if I could have my time again and make my decision again I'd have gone for a Ralt, but you can't do that . . .'

McNish had a Ralt with the Mugen engine and says, 'I think the Reynard chassis suited certain circuits and the Ralt chassis suited others. The Toyota had been very good the previous year and won the championship in a Reynard with JJ and Pacific Racing, so it was a pretty safe bet, but overall it wasn't as strong as a Ralt VW or Ralt Mugen. The Mugen was a little bit of a chance because it was the first time it had raced in the UK. We didn't know anything about it, and it took time to get the car developed and the engine working correctly.'

The 1989 Formula 3 season comprised 17 rounds, stretched from 27 March to 15 October, and included drivers of real ability, among them Rickard Rydell (Reynard-Spiess), Salo (Reynard-Alfa Romeo), Paul Stewart (Reynard-Mugen), Otto Rensing (Reynard-Mugen), Paul Warwick (Reynard-Toyota), and David Brabham (Ralt-Spiess). As a matter of record, 35 entries journeyed to Thruxton for the first round, and 21 had gone the Reynard route, 12 the Ralt route and one was with Dallara.

At Thruxton, Hakkinen qualified 16th and finished 15th. He was never near the pace and although he seemed to be going better at the next round, Silverstone – qualifying seventh and finishing ninth – he was disqualified for a minor infringement about his helmet. Round 3 was at Brands Hatch, and Dragon had been testing extensively there the week before. Hakkinen took pole and finished the race third.

McNish says that 'Mika put the car on pole a few times and led a few races, so I don't think you can ever say the car wasn't capable. Reynard did win races and he should have won a couple. Therefore Dragon wasn't a disaster but, for whatever reason, they didn't have a successful year.'

Absalom echoes it. 'We had a fairly disappointing year although there were some good highlights. We ran well in certain races.'

It might seem perverse to be into a retrospective examination of the season after only three of the 17 races, but I'm doing it partly to explain the rest of the season and partly to underscore how elusive getting it right in motor sport really is. The consequences of taking the wrong route with equipment can wrench the heart of any young driver. He knows how good he is, but he must spend from 27 March to 15 October largely unable to prove it. At Thruxton Hakkinen had been reduced to

With James Hunt, the man who helped so much (Erkki Mustakari, Finnpremio Oy/Ltd).

scrabbling with drivers far, far down the field in direct contrast to his Vauxhall-Lotus triumph at this same circuit only a few months before.

Silverstone. Qualified seventh. In the race he and Rensing made contact at Copse and plunged off. Hakkinen strode angrily back to the pits claiming that Rensing, a lap down after a pit stop, had 'closed the door' on him. Rensing, evidently, did not share the sentiments and these many years later chuckles about it, although he can't remember the crash itself.

'I remember Mika OK, although not the race in detail. Mika was a nice guy but sometimes a little bit over-enthusiastic. Of course, you are talking about young men – well, I was 27! The general atmosphere was one of competition but otherwise OK. For me it was a different situation: the first time in England, although a very nice time. I enjoyed England and racing there apart from my results. I think Mika thought about me as I thought about him: it would be good for our careers to beat the other one.'

Monaco. The traditional support race to the Grand Prix bringing together the best of Europe's hopefuls. This vintage included Jacques Villeneuve, Gianni Morbidelli and Karl Wendlinger. Hakkinen qualified 16th, although thereby hangs a tale. *Autosport* reported that 'one place behind [Eugenio] Visco [an Italian] was the driver who made the greatest one-lap-wonder of qualifying, Mika Hakkinen saving himself and Dragon from the ignominy of missing the cut with the final lap. For two laps, the crew signalled to Mika that he had a misfire but he didn't notice, and then came to a halt opposite the pits. Marshals pushed the car along to the end of the pit-lane and the team managed to reconnect the battery lead and return him to the fray with time for just two laps. He spun at Loews [the hairpin] and then improved by over 1.65 seconds on his final attempt!'

Hughie Absalom reflects that 'when we ran at Monaco we were so far out after the first qualifying session that we weren't even in the race. Then, in the second session, after a while he came by and he had a misfire. We thought *jeeez, that's it, we'd better pack up and go home*. We watched him go by and gave him the IN board and he didn't come in, he stayed out. The next time he comes along and the thing stops right in front of the pits and somehow or other a marshal pushed it across and into the pit exit.

'We went up there and pulled him back and we saw a terminal on the battery had broken. We put a new battery in it and we had about another 8 minutes of the session left. He went back out and qualified, came back in again and said *I had to drive like a madman*. Well, I think sometimes that's what it takes, and he had it. I did feel there was a precious talent there. I never worked with Senna so I don't know about him, but I have worked with a lot of other people and I am able to judge. There was definitely something special there.'

What would Hakkinen be like 'pressing on' if this was taking it easy?

About the pit board, Hakkinen says that 'maybe I didn't care. No, it's not right to say that I didn't care because of course I cared. I mean this in another way: I wasn't in the race and this was no time to go into the pits so I didn't care what they put on the board! That lap when I came out again [falls silent, feels for the words] . . . that was . . . [pauses again] . . . that was a terrible experience. I went over the edge and since then I've done it three more times. When you do things like that, you drive against the normal rules. You do things you should not do with a racing car. You're driving it wrong. You are like a madman. You don't care if you go into a corner sideways and no lifting off the accelerator. So you qualify, but 25th, 26th, and you think *did I risk all this for that?* Crazy. If you're qualifying to be first, you take a risk like that, it's different and I'm ready to do it – but 25th, 26th? Not worth it.'

You did it because you were young.

'Hmmm. I tell you, sometimes in a Formula 1 car these days on a qualifying lap you do similar things, go like mad, drive like crazy, sometimes over the edge – you always try and keep a car under your control, but that kind of lap is not under your control. As a result it is very dangerous and I don't like driving a car in that way. You can hurt yourself.'

An unspecial Formula 3 race in Monaco. Hakkinen held off Frenchman Laurent Daumet, but they crashed at the chicane. That cost Hakkinen four places and Daumet any chance of finishing – he'd twisted his hand in the steering wheel in the impact and his front wing was bent back on to one of his tyres. He limped to Rascasse – the tight turn before the start-finish straight – where marshals wrenched the wing off and presented it to him as, presumably, a souvenir. Daumet stalked into the pits and retired.

Brands Hatch (Indy Circuit). Pole. Hakkinen made a crisp start and established a constant lead of half a second over Brabham after five laps. Brabham and a driver called Derek Higgins began to close. Brabham darted at Hakkinen 'just to let him know I was there. I kept pushing and I made sure I was in the right position when we came up to lap the back-markers.' As Hakkinen tackled one of them, Brabham went round the outside of them both. Higgins tried, too, but later confessed, 'Yes, I made a hash of things. I noticed that Mika was looking jumpy when we came up to the back-markers, so I made my move. Unfortunately I wasn't positive enough. Still, at least I tried.' He bent his nosecone against Hakkinen.

Thruxton. Qualified 23rd, after he'd gone off at the chicane. 'I took the wrong line, went too wide and got on to the dust and could do nothing about spinning off backwards into the tyres.' That happened in the first session, and Dragon raced against time to repair the car for the second session. In the race he finished 12th after 'tigering' his way up the order. McNish won . . .

Silverstone. Qualified 38th, penalised because the car had its rear wing mounted 1mm too high. He was sent off to join the qualification race and with a 10-second penalty. He finished 19th. McNish won . . .

Donington. Qualified 16th, evidently baffled by the lack of speed that a new chassis was allowing him. Early in the race he ran seventh and later eighth after Paul Stewart overtook him. One report insists that Hakkinen was 'plainly still not happy with his car'. McNish won . . .

Silverstone. Qualified 15th. In the race he produced a storming drive from ninth on lap 2 to eventually challenging Robertson for fourth, putting pressure on him before deftly flicking out and getting by on the exit from the Woodcote complex. Hakkinen set off after Salo and cut the gap, cut the gap. With four laps left he moved past into Stowe corner.

'It was very hot and lots of people made the mistake of trying too hard early on and damaging the tyres,' Hakkinen explained. 'I took it

Right Spectacular Spa: Hakkinen doesn't lead into the Eau Rouge corner but won the race (Zooom, courtesy Vauxhall).

easy.' (Tony Dodgins, one of the reporters covering the race, wondered aloud quite what Hakkinen would be like 'pressing on' if this was what he meant by taking it easy.)

Mika finished fifth, raised to third when McNish and Brabham were disqualified for illegal engines.

Snetterton. Qualified front row. He seized the lead, Stewart in pursuit, but a Colombian, John Estupinan, went off at Sear, the awkward right-hander, spreading grass everywhere. 'I saw the grass and decided to brake earlier than normal,' Stewart said, 'but I noticed that Mika was braking as late as ever so I wasn't surprised when he spun there.' This spin dropped Hakkinen to sixth.

He was upside down in the air, his head coming for my head

Autosport reported that 'Hakkinen, in his angry attempt to make up ground, had a monster of a shunt. Class B runner Charles Rickett had rotated at the Bombhole, scattering tyres back on to the track. And, as they started to fall, Mika elected to drive around the outside. He missed Charles but was launched into a sequence of barrel-rolls when he hit the tyres, flying back over Charles and [John] Alcorn – getting so close to the latter that John's windscreen strip was found in Mika's cockpit! "People say that if I was 2 inches taller I wouldn't be here now," related Alcorn. "All I saw was his helmet, but not the expression on his face as he passed by." Hakkinen landed upside down but was able to climb out and stagger away, suffering dizziness and shock.' The race was stopped and the final positions settled at where the cars were running when the crash happened.

Alcorn remembers it well. 'It happened at the Bombhole just after the bridge. The Bombhole is a dipping right-hander where the camber initially works with you, then it works against you on the exit. It's one of those sorts of corners that the good guys in F3 or F3000 can take flat if they have a well-set-up car, and everyone else struggles and risks swiping the barriers. Certainly then, the barriers – tyre walls – were only about 6 or 7 feet from the edge of the track.

'Someone went off and clipped Mika, which sent him up into the air as I was coming round. I had to avoid the car that had hit the tyre wall

– it was bouncing out – so I went across the grass, *therefore* meeting Mika who, by this time, had rolled. He was upside down in the air and me the right way up. His head was coming for my head. I'm not sure if it was his roll bar or his helmet that took off one of my mirrors. I ducked and fortunately, being short, when I duck in a monocoque I can get my head beneath the top of it.

'That was the race Paul Stewart won backwards! He spun on the exit of the Russell chicane [feeding on to the start-finish straight] and did a 180-degrees. He went backwards up the straight and crossed the line like that. Because of the accident at the Bombhole and the race being stopped, Stewart won . . .'

I'm curious to know what happens when you've just had a crash like that and you've nearly been beheaded. Do you speak to the man afterwards?

'No. It is just one of those things. It happens, you accept it,' Alcorn says. 'To this day, one of the things that disappoints me with motor racing is that it is getting too safe. The more dangerous it is – from my own way of thinking, and I think Mika would probably subscribe to this, too – the more it sorts the men out from the boys: the guys that are prepared to take the risks and the ones that aren't. The bottom line is that if you are in single-seater racing, the majority of you are aiming for those 20-odd places on the Formula 1 grid and, without sounding macabre or whatever, you don't really care what happens to people as long as a space pops up for you.'

So is it survival of the fittest?

'You wouldn't have these big-budget rent-a-drive people who are at the back of the field if, quite frankly, it was still as dangerous as it used to be, because they'd be too frightened to do it.'

Hakkinen remembers running 'seventh or eighth after I spun. Funnily enough, the Bombhole is such a strange corner. The car gets very, very light at the entry to the corner, so you have little control, and when you come out of the corner the car gets light again. In other words, you don't have full control of the car. I went flat out through into the corner and Rickett spun at the exit. I thought *OK, I'm going to pass him on the outside, no problem, because it's the racing line*, but what he didn't do was put the brakes on. His car started rolling slowly backwards. I had to go wider and wider and wider so there was less and less room for me.

'It came to this: I didn't have time now to change and go the other way round him – if I had tried to do that, the car would be light up the hill and it wouldn't have turned in. I couldn't hit him because he would have died, for sure. His cockpit was right *there*. It was better to hit the wall, so I hit the wall – the barrier – and rolled back on to the track, hell of a shunt. Alcorn came round and I thought *Oh my God*.'

Discussing an incident like this, I'm curious to know the mental processes of the driver. First, it happens extremely fast in real time – but, to you, does it unfold slowly?

'Yes, quite slowly and there is time to think about what to do. You don't feel how hard the impacts really are. I don't know why you just don't feel it. You know what's going on, you hold the steering wheel as hard as you can, your neck as hard as you can, and you see what happens next. When the car stops you start looking around. Maybe you're upside down. The next thing is you're scared in case anybody else crashes into you; you're on a circuit upside down, anybody can hit you, so you're looking and the cars are going *whaam, whaam, whaam* past you. Next moment fuel is leaking and water is leaking and everything is leaking and you think *this can explode any second*. So then in one sense you panic. I've said I never panic but I do sometimes! [Smile, gentle laugh] So what happens after that? You think *I have got to get out of this car*. You take the seat belt off because you've forgotten in the middle of all this that you are upside down and *clunk* you fall [mimics hitting head on ground], *but* your body is being held by the steering wheel. You have to start taking the steering wheel off upside down, you're hanging there by your legs and you're thinking *what a disaster . . .*'

From this terrible motion that is out of control, this crash, when do you begin to think logically again?

'The moment the car stops. Before that, you cannot do anything.'

One time at Hockenheim I saw Niki Lauda have a tremendous crash in qualifying at the first corner, climb out of the cockpit and run away from the wreckage. Normal human reaction, I thought. Wrong. Lauda, of course, was running back to the pits to get in the spare car because he knew there was still time for a fast lap or two.

'I had a shunt in qualifying at Hockenheim in the Lotus, 1991 – first corner, too. Only thing I do, I take the steering wheel off and I am running back towards the pits for the spare car. While I am running

The portrait of 1988 (Zooom, courtesy Vauxhall).

back I think *hell of a shunt*. Only when I am running back. *Yes, hell of a shunt, but I need to qualify, I need to get in the spare car.* That's it – you push a car to its limit and it's going to happen. It's normal.'

Has it ever crossed your mind that ordinary people don't reason like that and can't reason like that?

'In motor racing you have shunts. Always will have shunts. I will still in my life have many shunts. I cannot help it. I hope they are not big ones, I hope they are going to be small ones, but any driver – any driver in the world – will have shunts sooner or later.'

What mechanism do you use to accept this?

'It's terrible, but you just have to. Don't think about them but prepare yourself for them because one day they will happen.'

How can you prepare yourself without thinking about them?

[Long pause] 'Somehow psychologically because, as I have just said, I know it will happen but I do not have to think about that all the time. It could be a mechanical failure, not your mistake. I've had three Grands Prix so far this year [1997], and it's been going fantastically: no spins, no accidents – well, spins but no accidents, nothing. I feel I've been driving really well, but every driver will have the big shunt and you know that.'

Oulton. Qualified fourth. He ran fourth until a fuel pipe broke and he was reduced to a crawl to the line, sixth.

Silverstone. Qualified 17th, struggling for balance. He finished 10th.

Brands Hatch. Qualified second, 'happy enough because there was so much traffic and I started to misfire when the car ran low on fuel near the end.' He nursed real hopes of winning the race but finished sixth: he found the car 'creeping' before the green light, got bogged down when the green did come on and was enveloped from behind.

Donington. Qualified 10th. At the hairpin on the opening lap of the race a Portuguese, Antonio Simoes, made a self-confessed 'bad mistake. My clutch was slipping and when I put the car into first again it shot back on to the track. I hit Mika. I'm sorry.'

Silverstone. Qualified 20th. Because the full Grand Prix circuit was being used and the Toyota runners were at a power disadvantage, he finished 11th after a 'disappointing run'.

Thruxton. Qualified 19th. He finished the race, the final round of the championship, 12th.

'From the middle of the season on, it was getting hard work,' Absalom says, 'not least because Allan McNish was doing so well with Dick Bennetts. Mika was probably looking back and thinking *God, I should have done that deal.* It was a sense of all-round disappointment. There were days when it was difficult. He was very headstrong and if you tried to control him – if you didn't do all the right things to control him – then it was quite difficult. To be headstrong is, in hindsight, perhaps a good thing, but it never is at the time! Again using hindsight, I am sure he relished how hard that season was for him.'

Relished?

'Yes, in his own little way, yes, because he came through it and he learned about disappointment a long time before he got to Formula 1. I guess the same thing happened to him when he did get into Formula 1

Right *Making the best of 1989 in Formula 3* (Zooom).

at Lotus. Motivation is a very hard thing to keep up if you are not running where you are normally used to running, at the front.'

I asked for an evaluation of Hakkinen the driver. 'He's like Ronnie Peterson was. Given a good car, he's very, very quick, but if you're trying to figure out something I don't think he's able to do that. Mika comes out of the same grouping as Peterson. Although he likes to know what's going on he hasn't got the engineering ability to identify various small things.'

Or the approach that Senna had, analysing a problem until whatever hour of the night it took to find a solution?

'Mika is not that way inclined. Mind you, there aren't very many who are . . .'

Hakkinen, reflecting on the year, says, 'It was weird, it was weird because now when I think about it, what seemed the wrong decision then was in fact the right decision. I don't think I would be sitting here today [April 1997 in Monaco] if I had not made that decision. I learned. One thing I learned very heavily was how fast things can change. OK, in 1988 I had had a championship, I'd been racing very closely with Allan. In 1989, *whooosh*, it was gone. Three races and I was at the back of the grid. I was thinking *what happened to me? Have I changed?* I looked in the mirror. *I haven't changed, so what's going on?* I understood how important it is to have a good package: good engine, good car. I do not want to say that that year Dragon were a crap team, it was just that they were not ready. Looking back, my bad year – my failing year – was a good year. I've had a lot of bad years [chuckle].

'Actually, at the end of the day it's not too difficult to cope with. It depends how you take it. If you start living with self-pity you start looking in the mirror and seeing a face [lowers voice] saying *I'm no good, why do these things happen to me?* You start living with these feelings and you are going to go down – and then it is difficult. But if you fight – and I don't care how long it takes, one year, two years, ten years, 50 years – but you're going to fight, fight, fight every day to be better, and that's the only way you can do it, fighting it, fighting it one day at a time.'

One race remained in 1989, a non-Championship Formula 3 event called the Cellnet Superprix at Brands Hatch in late October.

'What happened was fortuitous from my point of view and fortuitous from Mika's point of view,' McNish says, setting out the background: a jigsaw puzzle where all the pieces suddenly interlocked. 'Obviously the pressure was on Mika because he had had such a strong year in Vauxhall-Lotus and he had shown signs of *dragging* a lot of speed, but he hadn't been able to hold that together in Formula 3.'

The pieces:

JJ Lehto, in Formula 3000 with the Pacific team, was moving up. He had signed to drive the tail-end of the season with ONYX in Formula 1, and would be at the Japanese Grand Prix, Suzuka, on 22 October.

Why bother with debriefs asked Mika – 'We're quickest, what's the problem?'

McNish, in Formula 3 with West Surrey Racing, was moving up. He had 'agreed to take JJ's seat' at the final F3000 round, Dijon, on the same day as the Japanese Grand Prix. 'Consequently it meant that my Formula 3 seat at West Surrey was vacant for the Cellnet Superprix. And there was Mika . . .'

In effect, McNish summarises, everyone 'climbed a rung' on their career ladders.

'It was a Marlboro pressure thing, really,' Absalom says. 'They believed Mika was better than his results had been showing. The way round it was to give him a ride with Dick at West Surrey, and that's what happened. Allan went off to do the Formula 3000 race.'

Round the Indy circuit at Brands – which is the Grand Prix circuit without the long loop into the trees out of sight – Hakkinen exploited West Surrey's competitive car to the full. He had tested with the team the week before and 'my motivation came straight back. The car is good and the engine is good, but it is the whole package that is important.' He was the only driver to reach into the 42 seconds (at 42.89, Brabham next, 43.02).

Bennetts spreads the background. 'It all started through Keke, because I'd run Keke when I worked for Fred Opert [American Chevron importer and race entrant] and we talked about it. We'd discussed it at the end of 1988, because Marlboro – with McNish and Hakkinen – finished 1–2 in England and 1–2 in Europe [well, 1–3 in Europe, but never mind]. As it worked out, Allan came to us in 1989 and he was very happy. We got Mika for this one race through Marlboro, but we wanted to run him. Allan had the opportunity to do the 3000 race so we said *Allan moves on and does that, we'll put Mika into Allan's car. All we've got to do is a seat fitting.* We went to Snetterton, gave him half a day to get comfortable, and we did the Superprix at Brands.

Below and overleaf *The Bombhole bomburst at Snetterton. Photographer Barry Ambrose was behind the barrier and saw Hakkinen coming straight for him. 'There wasn't really time to do anything except duck,' he says. 'The car struck more or less directly in front of me. When I looked up there was so much dust everywhere that I could hardly see anything and if you look carefully at the picture of Mika crawling out it is slightly fuzzy – the dust still hadn't settled.'*

'Mika was so green. We had a Friday afternoon session and he was quickest. I had watched him in the Dragon at Brands in the wet [the third round in April] and it was just big balls that kept him as quick as he was. The car was undrivable! When he got in our car at the Cellnet Superprix it was also wet and he was happier being quickest in those circumstances than actually getting pole because he was quicker than David Brabham,

who was recognised to be the rainmaster. However, session over, at about 5 minutes past 5 Mika wanted to go home! We had the split transporter: hospitality unit in the front, workshop in the rear. I took him to the front and gave him a blank map of the circuit. I said *right, you fill that in with what the car's doing.* I've found over the years it helps us and also concentrates a driver's mind on thinking what he is doing.

'I said *right, I'll go out and see how the lads are doing preparing the car for tomorrow, and you fill in the map.* I was away for about 15 minutes, and when I came back the map was still blank. I learned, and it was an embarrassment for the poor kid, that he couldn't write anything, couldn't put it down in words in English [because his command of the language was not yet good enough]. I said *come on,* but he just couldn't do it.

'I said *right, you describe it to me and I'll fill in the map. Sit your bum down here and let's talk about this.* Mika said *we're quickest, what's the problem?* I explained that there was no problem but if we talk about it we can learn. *But why? I'm quickest.* I explained that he might have been able to go even quicker. I had a friend helping out doing corner times and he said Mika was sideways through Paddock. I said *Mika, you've got a bit of oversteer.* He said *it's OK!* Mika explained everything with his hands. [At this point Bennetts illustrates this by holding an imaginary steering wheel and turning it this way and that to demonstrate oversteer, understeer.] And he'd wanted to disappear out the door 5 minutes after the session ended! I think that's what he thought motor racing was. *OK, I'm happy, let's go home and come back tomorrow.*'

I muse that if people are naturally talented, they can behave like that.

'Yes, but it was raw talent. Anyway, we eventually decided to make some changes if it was dry on the Saturday, and he went quicker again . . .'

Hakkinen draws a 'very clear difference between West Surrey Racing against Dragon. West Surrey Racing was professional, organised and I knew the team was good. I was unbelievably confident when I went with them for that race. It was the first time I had been with a big team – well, Dragon was a big team, just not professional. I knew I was going to win. The car was – the word perfect may be wrong but I loved it, loved it! How the car handled. I was able to drive so fast it was unbelievable. Also I had had this bad season and I knew how important the race was, mega-important, for next year's contract. I hadn't had good results so I needed that result. I decided to go for it, put everything into it. This was different to that crazy lap at Monaco. This was controlled speed. Fantastic, the feeling, fantastic.'

Autosport wrote of the start of the race: 'Hakkinen had his eyes firmly fixed on the green light, and began to roll. He checked it, just as they flicked on, and struggled to beat Brabham to the first corner, but he managed it even if it meant sliding wide on to the old circuit [after the first corner, where a strip of tarmac runs alongside the 'new' circuit up towards the Druids loop]. Brabham saw his chance. "Mika came hard into Paddock still hard on the power so I went wide and let him by. As we slid out I tucked in and dragged by him on the hill to Druids."'

Brabham was the first of the front-runners to pit, on lap 21, but trying to accelerate away couldn't get first gear. Hakkinen pitted next lap and was stationary for 9.82 seconds. It settled the race and, enjoying this second set of tyres more than he had enjoyed the first, Hakkinen stretched his lead over Brabham to 8 seconds, winning at a canter. The gesture of his upraised arm and fist as he crossed the line was a release from the heart-wrenching that had gone before.

He drives on his wits, and has a natural feel for where the car and its limit is

---

'Of course I'm happy,' he said immediately afterwards. 'I started from pole, set fastest lap [a new lap record] and won the race. All year I have had bad results with another team chassis and engine. I had the opportunity to run with Dick and it was brilliant. We did the job properly in the pits and made no mistakes. I came in gently while all the others came in nearly flat. A little care was all that was needed.'

Today, Hakkinen adds to that. I explain that Bennetts thought he would win. 'I didn't think about what other people were thinking. I just thought I *can do it*. The car was good, the engine was good, I liked the team, I liked the mechanics, and I was proving to myself that, even after the sort of season that I had had, I could still do it.'

Absalom wasn't surprised. Don't forget, he points out, that 'the race was at Brands, where Mika had sat on pole twice for us, so really it was inevitable he was going to be good!'

'Yes, Mika won that race,' McNish says, 'which gave him a lot of confidence. I think he had lost all confidence through the year and was disappointed. We were still pretty young at that point, you know, just driving along doing our thing, but I do feel that in a career there is a lot about momentum and confidence through all the formulae as you rise. Formula 3 is the first where you have to think, use your brain. You can't

Out on the Oulton circuit testing the tyres, and inset preparing for the test in June 1989 (Ian Simpson).

just drive on brawn. You've got to use your brain as well to work on the set-ups, and that was especially true that year in Formula 3 because it was the first year of radial tyres. Therefore it was fresh to everyone. To get into a car and have a really good run at the end of the season built his confidence up again, and he was ready for the following year.

'He drives on his wits. He has a natural feeling for where the car and its limit is. He has had to change, because he is a different driver to the one he was when I raced against him last, in Formula 3. He has had to

think about it more, learn the technical side a bit more. I think that now with David Coulthard at McLaren [1996–97] there is a good balance, in that Mika is exceptionally fast over one lap but David is more of a thinker; he can work with the car and the team perhaps a little bit better – although I know the team respect Mika enormously.'

Because he is bloody quick?

'He is quick, he is quick. What he has managed to do lately is be more consistent. When he had off days before, they were pretty bad and he wasn't able to keep the consistency there. Mind you, this was six or seven years ago, and naturally he has developed since then. I remember one instance where he had just stuck the car on pole at

With Mika Sohlberg, here in 1990 (Erkki Mustakari, Finnpremio Oy/Ltd).

Zandvoort and, on the slowing-down lap, he drove off the circuit because he had lapsed in concentration. You know, he'd shown enough speed to take pole and then gone off; but, I repeat, we were both pretty young and he's tempered that now.'

What McNish says next is of particular interest because it seems to contradict what Hakkinen has already said, McNish taking care of a lot of business, Hakkinen simply driving. I suspect that the difference between the two positions was not as stark as it might appear. Anyway, McNish says: 'Looking back, I am sure we simply went out and enjoyed our motor racing. I certainly enjoyed my year in Vauxhall-Lotus and my year in Formula 3, although I'm not sure that Mika could honestly say he enjoyed his year in Formula 3 before he joined Dick. The weight of the world was not exactly on our shoulders, and certainly not the way it is now for drivers at a similar stage. That's because of the way things have developed. Every driver is expected to bring sponsorship to allow him to go motor racing, and that wasn't really the same for us. There was Marlboro, there was Camel, there were many other sponsors

– Opel Team Holland, Opel Team Germany, there was Yokohama – a tremendous amount of sponsorship coming in. Between then and now we are talking about different pressures on the driver.'

Meaning it is much more difficult for him to enjoy himself?

'Entirely correct. It relates to what I said about the confidence. If you don't have that it's hard to pull the best out of yourself and, consequently, you are not enjoying it.'

Confidence restored, and with a full season of West Surrey Racing beckoning, Mika Hakkinen fully intended to enjoy himself in 1990, but before that he had a last race for Dragon, the wonderful and notorious Macau Grand Prix in November. Like the Monaco support race, it attracted a broad spectrum of young (and youngish) bulls. This vintage, for instance, included Julian Bailey and Schumacher. Hakkinen qualified 15th, not helped by clipping a wall.

At the start of heat 1 there was the traditional locking of horns – a huge crash, this one involving Rydell, Rensing, McNish, Irvine and others. The crash offered Hakkinen a second chance, because on the parade lap his gearbox had failed and he could only find one gear. The Dragon team changed gearboxes and he finished 14th. In heat 2 *this* gearbox failed at the start.

Alcorn provides a footnote: 'I didn't know Mika before that 1989 season and, to start off with, he didn't really count, wasn't a threat. All the winter testing I'd been favourite and I'd been quickest at all the pre-season tests.' Alcorn would experience engine difficulties although both he and Hakkinen were using Toyotas. 'At any fast tracks Mika wasn't very quick, but as soon as he got to places like Oulton Park and Brands Hatch – which, I believed, required a lot more driver skill – suddenly as far as I was concerned he was the closest one to me. He would chuck the car around, be aggressive with it, and at those sort of tracks you can overcome slight chassis or engine deficiencies or whatever.

'I didn't really get to know him personally, no, for the simple reason that I was one of those people who didn't socialise with someone that I considered a threat: a fellow competitor. Still to this day I don't understand how racing drivers can be sociable to one another. It's contrary to where it's at. I think Mika was slightly the same. He was a bit of a loner, concentrating 100 per cent on what he was doing and sod everybody else. To me that's correct.'

• CHAPTER THREE •

Profit and loss

FOR 1990 HAKKINEN joined Bennetts and West Surrey Racing. 'Of course, Keke knew how we operated,' Bennetts says, 'and he was annoyed that Mika didn't come to us in 1989. He said to me *Hakkinen for you in 1990 with or without Marlboro money. I'll find the money if Marlboro don't.* So that was how it was. Did we want him? Oh yes. I rated him. Allan McSwishy [a McNickname for McNish, I assume] was good, but with Mika you could see the natural talent and he was relaxed' – which the naturally talented can afford to be.

'We used to have to wake him up before a race. He'd be sleeping in the hospitality unit – 15 minutes to go and you'd say *come on, Haka,* and he'd make those sort of groaning noises people make when they are coming out of a deep sleep. You get other guys who are the reverse of that. Take the Osvaldo Negri scenario [Negri, a Brazilian whom West Surrey ran in 1992]. Once when he had pole at Silverstone he would not leave the garage and he would not let anyone touch that car. He was paranoid 'cos he's on pole and *don't touch the car, it's perfect.* We needed to explain that certain work had to be done, checking the tyre pressures, change the battery, put fuel in. *No, don't touch it!* Mika would just wander off, he wouldn't care less. He'd simply leave it to us, and that was the difference. Mika was so confident. We do our job preparing the car, he does his job driving it. The problem was that you'd sit him down and go through the list: engine, gearbox, brakes. He'd always shrug his shoulders and say *no, it's all good.* That didn't make it easy for us. In fact that was difficult.'

In making these judgements, of course, Bennetts is coming in at a level far above simply winning races, which he and his team had been doing for a long time, not least in taking Senna to the Formula 3 championship, as I have said. By 1990 Bennetts was wise in the ways of every aspect of the Formula and could anticipate his drivers progressing eventually to Formula 1.

An articulate and organised Australian lady called Suzanne Radbone was working for Bennetts, although she'd arrived by a roundabout route. She'd been 'in the Grand Prix office in Adelaide for five years and I met Joe Saward [a British journalist who said that if she ever reached England she could lodge with him]. I came over on the understanding from Ian Phillips [former journalist then working for the Leyton House team] that I would go to work for him up at Bicester, but I was also offered a job by John Dunbar at the Zooom photographic agency.

'It was a toss up, but I decided to work for Zooom in Fulham. I stayed there for about a year but the job wasn't quite what I thought it would be so I looked around. It might even have been Joe or it might have been the people at Jardine PR – which Zooom did a lot of work for – who suggested I contacted Dick Bennetts because he was looking for somebody. I contacted Dick and after a little while of Dick humming and hawing – which is standard procedure for Dick – he finally offered me the job.'

Bennetts described this job as Suzanne sitting at the front desk at the team's offices keeping everything under control and keeping the unwanted at bay. Suzanne amplifies it by adding that her duties included 'doing his accounts, his travel arrangements, and some sponsorship proposals. I went with the team and that was my introduction to circuits. I first met Mika when he arrived early in 1990 to have a look at the car at the workshop [adjoining the offices]. He came with a close friend of his, Mika Sohlberg – they'd been friends for quite some time, they were practically joined at the hip! Mika is the sort of person who always needs to have someone around him and, because Sohlberg decided to spend a couple of years in London, it worked out quite well.'

'Through the passage of time' Radbone would become a maternal figure, organising Hakkinen, who was completely disorganised. We shall see.

'Mika was never very keen on testing,' she says. 'I had to make his arrangements and try to track him down to tell him what was happening. The situation was difficult sometimes. I don't think Mika's command of English at that point was all that brilliant, but I don't know how much [of not understanding] he chose to put on and how much he just couldn't understand. People couldn't emphasise enough to him the importance of English. Even then he had his own ideas of what was and what was not important – things like testing. He was not interested in testing. Just racing. He was just a racer. Couldn't be bothered with any of the rest of it, much to Dick's dismay. To Dick, and later on Peter Collins at Lotus, trying to teach Mika to be a test driver was almost a full-time occupation for them, but he just wasn't interested.' (Hakkinen: 'It's different if there is something new to try out, but just going round and round . . .')

I venture that perhaps it was because Hakkinen had so much natural talent that he felt he didn't need to be interested.

'I think that was Mika's belief,' she says. 'He believed that, given a competitive car, he would win. The rest of it was trivial and he didn't see that it was necessary, much to the disappointment of his team managers. That's what I mean about his belief, where sometimes he chose not to speak English very well or not to take directions very well. He didn't see it as necessary.'

What do you think about that, what's your position on that?

'I think it was probably a combination of both [belief in himself, unbelief in the unnecessary]. There was an arrogance in his own belief that was very good and it certainly was a well-founded belief, but there is another side to Mika that really couldn't be bothered. He was certainly enthusiastic to a point, but beyond that other things crept in that he felt were more important. They were a distraction. His attention span – and I don't mean this in a cruel way – to things like testing was, well, he'd do it and at that certain point he'd think *I'm bored now.* Round and round and round a circuit to him is not anything to get excited about. Thruxton and Silverstone and Snetterton were Mika's most dreaded places for testing' – because there were a lot of races there, a lot of testing there and he knew every inch of such as Snetterton backwards, to coin an unfortunate phrase for everyone except Paul Stewart.

I don't want you to gain an immediate impression that Suzanne Radbone is being clinically critical. Her truthfulness is based on great affection and great honesty. She will have a great deal more to say, and all of it will be affectionate and honest, too. You see the way it is:

The triumphant season of 1990 with Dick Bennetts and West Surrey Racing. This is Hakkinen in first qualifying at Oulton Park (Ian Simpson).

disliking Mika Hakkinen is extremely difficult, and if there are sharp edges to this book, there are sharp edges to every life.

The 1990 season stretched from April until October, embracing 17 rounds, and Hakkinen's main rival would be Salo. Some highlights:

By the time they reached round 8 at Silverstone in early June, Hakkinen had won three times, Salo four. At Silverstone, Peter Collins of the Lotus Formula 1 team watched fascinated. 'Hakkinen had been embroiled in a very hectic dice with Salo and the two of them touched ever so lightly in the Complex [the tortuous and twisty section before the start-finish straight]. Hakkinen went off, hit the guard rail and that finished his race, but what impressed me was that they had raced through a medium-speed left-hand corner absolutely wheel-to-wheel within an inch of one another and didn't touch. They left room for one another despite the fact that they were on the limit. That impressed me: the judgement and the car control that you need to be able to do

91

that confidently. It said a great deal, especially in the Complex where you normally say *OK, I'll follow you through*. Hakkinen went off just because he got on the power hard coming out of the corner in an attempt to get or keep an advantage. The car simply got away from him, but I was impressed, yes I was.'

Collins would not forget what he had seen both men do. Hakkinen says, 'It was quite an interesting moment. I had a problem with the car at the time; I always seemed to have a problem with the car at Silverstone. I never did have a good set-up there until the end of the season, when I was mega-quick. Mid-season I wasn't so quick and I was fighting with Salo. I went off just because we were side-by-side fighting for the position and I had the car on the limit.'

During my 1997 interview, I pointed out to Hakkinen that Collins remembered it.

'Positively?' Hakkinen was anxious to know.

Yes, positively.

Surveying that season, Bennetts says, 'It was very competitive because of Mika Salo, it was really just the two of them.' Steve Robertson, Bennetts adds, had a disastrous time early on, but 'beat us round Silverstone' – the same round 8 when Hakkinen went off in the Complex.

Marlboro naturally wanted to capitalise on the publicity potential of West Surrey Racing and Hakkinen. They persuaded Bennetts to enter a round in each of the Italian, French and German Formula 3 Championships, respectively at Imola on 17 June, Dijon on 22 July and Hockenheim on 13 October. Hakkinen won Imola comfortably enough, but back in Britain for round 9 at Donington 'was when Mika had the off weekend. He just wasn't on the pace,' Bennetts says. 'He was having problems with a lady friend and didn't let on to me. Fortunately a good chum of his, Mika Sohlberg, helped us an incredible amount that weekend because if we'd believed our Mika and what he was saying, we'd have torn that car completely apart trying to find something wrong with it.'

Christian Fittipaldi, Bennetts's other driver, took pole because, as Bennetts said, 'we decided not to use a lap board. Christian was very good and honest for his age and he said *I'm overdriving it because I see P3* [you're third quickest] *and I try harder to be P1 and I make a mistake, go to P4*. So I said OK, we'll fix that, no pit board for places, just minutes of the session remaining – nothing else on the board. Christian got pole because he drove within himself. I said we'd do the same with Mika, but no, he wanted everything on his board, his time, the fastest time, everything.'

Hakkinen qualified fourth.

'I said to Sohlberg,' Bennetts recounts, 'we've stripped the car as far as we dare and Neil Brown [the engine man] says he can't find anything wrong with the engine. Nor could we find anything wrong with the chassis. We said to Mika *look, we are reluctant to change much. The car is as per the test day we had last Monday when you were quickest.* Christian was quick and happy with his car on the test day, P3, but he didn't push it, he used his head.

'On the Sunday morning Sohlberg told me *Mika's got a problem and the phone was going at the hotel at 3.30 in the morning from this woman.* Mika hadn't slept properly, he was away with the fairies, and in the race he drove like an idiot. He fought with Salo for fifth place. I joked with the pair of them: *you've come out in sympathy with each other because you're Finns! Normally you're on the front row of the grid, this weekend you're hovering round on the third row, and if one of you is there the other*

Keke Rosberg, the guiding hand – seen here with Nigel Mansell.

certainly shouldn't be! I have no idea what problem Salo had.'

It couldn't, I venture naughtily, have been the same woman . . .?

Bennetts [loud laughter]: 'I never thought of that one . . .'

Hakkinen: 'The girl? No, I don't want to talk about it . . .'

Anyway, after the race, which Fittipaldi won, Bennetts said to Hakkinen, 'Look, we know you have some problems. Forget this weekend and let's look to the next race.'

That was at Silverstone and won by Salo, Hakkinen second. West Surrey Racing then travelled to Dijon for their guest appearance in the French Formula 3 Championship, but the French made it clear that they weren't welcome and raised a lot of niggling obstacles like refusing a place in the paddock. Bennetts said *let's go home*, and they did.

With the help of a lot of people I got out of Immigration the same day

---

Hakkinen's absolute concentration on racing but lukewarm interest in details beyond racing now gave Bennetts a nightmare. 'We were so close to losing the Championship. The Thursday before a race at Snetterton [round 11 on 5 August, Hakkinen trailing Salo 61–72] – well, the Thursday evening, and bear in mind we had a session on the Friday morning, I got a call. It was 9.30, maybe 10.0.' The conversation . . .

A flat voice: 'Immigration, Terminal Two, Heathrow Airport.'

Bennetts: 'Yes?'

The voice: 'Mr Bennetts?'

Bennetts: 'Yes.'

The voice: 'Do you know a Mr Mika Hakkinen?'

Bennetts: 'Yes. Why?'

The voice: 'We are about to put him on a plane back to Finland.'

Bennetts: 'Why?'

The voice: 'Well, we have warned him since March the 8th that he needs a visa and he hasn't got one [Finland being outside the European Union]. He has come in and out several times and we have warned him . . .'

Bennetts ruminates that it was an example of Hakkinen thinking *you know, what's a piece of paper, what's the problem?*, and it had come to a head the Thursday night before a race meeting. 'I had to bend hell and

94

high water to convince immigration to let him in, *please let him stay until Monday, when he will leave the country.* It worked and we got him to Snetterton.'

So what happened?

'I never forget that because it was so crazy,' Hakkinen says. 'It was all about one stamp on my passport. Every time they stamped my passport. I used to go England-Finland, Finland-England, back and forwards all the time, stamp, stamp, stamp, and I didn't care what stamp they were putting on it. One day they put on a stamp – I can't remember exactly – that said *if you stay here longer than three months you're in trouble.* It was stamped like that and one day the immigration officer said *what's this stamp over here?* I said *what the hell, it's full of stamps!* He said *take a seat,* and he rang Dick Bennetts. I took the seat and I was sitting there four hours. Then the hassle started because I needed to race, I was near the Championship, it was important, I was in immigration and they were saying *you can't race, go back to Finland.* So that was it. With the great help of a lot of people I got out of that immigration the same day.'

Meanwhile, Bennetts says that 'the rules said he had to leave the country on Sunday night or first flight Monday morning and not return until he had a visa, which took four to six weeks to get. And the next race was a week away at Oulton. We faced a problem, a big problem. We had to get Rosberg involved, we had to get the Finnish Embassy involved and the British Embassy in Finland, we had to get Marlboro's solicitors involved. A lot of work was done to obtain a special dispensation to get him back in again the following Friday. He had to drive from Heathrow to Oulton Park. He arrived at 4.30 in the afternoon and the session finished at 5.0.

'He hopped in the car and bedded in a set of brake pads, then right, out he goes at 10 to 5, goes P1: no pit stops, no adjustments. We'd done two new developments with Christian on his car during the day, which were positive, so we put them on Mika's car and that was all. Steve Robertson's dad came down and said *we're wasting our time, aren't we?* [he put it more pungently, but never mind]. *That bloke's just arrived, we didn't even think he was coming because we'd heard he had immigration problems, he goes out and he's quickest.* And Mika himself? He shrugged his shoulders. OK, *what's the fuss?* He got the visa a couple of weeks after.'

Hakkinen remembers 'putting my overalls on quickly, putting my shoes on quickly – hardly had time to do up the laces – and I jumped in the car . . .'

Bennetts reflects that sometimes Hakkinen 'tried to portray the image that he was perfect and never went drinking. Christian was so candid with us. He'd say *Oh, we've been to a nightclub last night and cor, we got drunk*. I'd ask Mika how the nightclub was and he'd say [deadpan] *it was OK*. I'd ask if he's had a few drinks. *Oh no, no, no, no, no!* And really they were just young kids, they were enjoying themselves.

'The Sunday night after Mika won the Championship at Donington in September [he finished first in the race, Salo third], they went to a nightclub in London and got absolutely out of control. I rang Monday morning and Christian had crashed out on the floor of the flat of the two Mikas, Hakkinen and Sohlberg. Christian said *Oooh dear, I've got a headache*, but Mika said *Oh no, we didn't drink too much*. Why did he say that? I think he just didn't want to let me think he was wild.'

This is interesting, just as so many aspects of Hakkinen are.

'I remember that night very well,' he says. 'We had a good night – because I'd won the Championship at Donington. Christian Fittipaldi, Christian's friend Rodrigo and me and my friend Sohlberg went out in London to celebrate. Goddammit, I had just won the Championship. I don't remember the next day, but Christian was definitely lying on the floor holding his head. We had fun, good fun.'

But you wouldn't admit this.

'I don't know. I think alcohol doesn't suit car racing, anyway. To a driver, alcohol is not part of the business. I don't know. Partly it's the mentality of Finland that we have.'

I mean, here [Monaco, 1997] a glass of white wine is only a glass of white wine.

'In Finland we don't have that. It is a different mentality.'

Meaning in Finland, as in the other Scandinavian countries, alcohol is an escape from the cold and the winter darkness, a sort of annihilation of the present, but only if you drink yourself into oblivion – as they do. In Hakkinen's case I wonder if it was not something altogether different: a young man trying to be a mature man by denying he got drunk.

'Maybe, maybe. Yes, I think . . . no, I don't know. I cannot answer it. I also think this is partly my private life, which you don't want to share with anybody.'

They went to Hockenheim for their guest appearance in the German

Formula 3 Championship with no idea what to expect. 'Mika had raced at the circuit in Vauxhall-Lotus, but we hadn't been there so it was new to us,' Bennetts says. 'I set the car up for Hockenheim with Imola springs, roll bars and ride heights as a starting point. What else could we do? The Friday untimed session was a disaster. We had a misfire, the gear ratios were wrong and we were 22nd quickest. I don't know what his name was, but some smarmy German journalist came up and said *Ah, so much for this top British team, these British champions.* I said we had a few problems. Mika couldn't really help.

'Friday evening after first qualifying we were sixth quickest, still with a misfire, still with the wrong ratios.' Hakkinen had covered only four laps and that Friday night the team 'went through and changed all we could'. They'd taken the car of Minoru Tanaka, Bennetts's third driver, as a spare car. 'I was on the phone to England – you know, Neil was doing the engines and he'd stayed at home – asking *what can it be?* We went through everything and we finally changed everything out of Tanaka's car right down to the tail light. I said to the guys *change it all and then we're covered.* That car ran with no misfire in England so something strange happened, but we'd gone

By 1990 Hakkinen was becoming well known and attracting autograph hunters (Ian Simpson).

through two sessions and hadn't cured it. It was pit stop, pit stop every two laps.

'We had to try and learn the track and cure the misfire. We'd put new plugs in and Mika would do half a lap clean and it'd go wrong. I said I thought it was something to do with the fuel. The new plugs made it run clean, but when he'd been through the chicanes – off and on the throttle – it was fouling: too rich. How did Mika take this sort of thing? It concerned him and you could see that in his face because he wanted to win.

'As it turned out, it was the fuel potentiometer [an instrument for measuring or adjusting small amounts of electricity] that had failed. We'd never set one up before. Here's us at 10 o'clock Friday night, it was getting bloody cold and we said *right, let's go through it all again, this is the last chance.*

The very first F1 lap I did, I saw the mechanics running away from the pit wall

---

'There was also the problem of downforce because of the chicanes' – which are very fast at Hockenheim and, of course, contoured by kerbing. The fastest way is by bouncing over them because the shortest distance between two points is, truly, a straight line. 'The Vauxhall-Lotus being soft, by comparison, you could ride the kerbs easily. We had run our Formula 3 car at Imola like a go-kart, stiff, but Hockenheim with a stiff car? That was hard on the suspension, and a lot of cars failed with broken rockers and push-rods, but it was the only way to go quick. You had to straight-line it. That meant we needed to change the set-up a lot.'

A further problem in changing everything meant 'taking the fuel pot off the spare car and mounting it on the race car. We were on the phone to Neil [who wasn't at Hockenheim] and he'd say *turn it round 3 degrees*, but how do we know what 3 degrees is? Actually it was the width of a pencil. We set it up and that cured it. Saturday morning Mika went out on the old rubber, did a lap, came past the pits thumbs up, misfire cured. He came in, we put new rubber on, he went out and *whaam*: 2m 08.35s.'

A certain Michael Schumacher responded with 2m 09.36 and a certain Otto Rensing responded with 2m 10.19s.

'What happened at Hockenheim?' Rensing muses, his voice rising through the repetition. 'Hakkinen came there and he was bloody quick, he was. He was bloody quick and it was fantastic because he really brought everything out of Michael and myself. I remember the situation: we were doing practice times around 2m 12s, something like this, and Mika came and did the 08s and suddenly Michael was down into the 09s and I was in the 10s – which we never thought possible until Mika showed us what could be done. I would never have believed it if someone had told me I'd do a 10s. I'd have said *no, not possible, sorry but I can't do it.* The situation with Michael was the same. Both of us did something we never, never would have believed before.

'Mika had the best car and the best team and he got the feeling of winning. I know this feeling, although it's a very long time ago [chuckle]: you are so relaxed and you say OK *there is nobody who can beat me*, and this makes you even quicker. That was what Mika had.'

In the race Hakkinen produced a paralysing exhibition. At the end of the opening lap he led Schumacher by 1.1 seconds. Wolfgang Schattling, a noted reporter on German Formula 3, wrote in *Autosport*: 'There was no catching Hakkinen while those behind squabbled. Rensing demoted Schumacher on lap 3, Schumacher regained the place a lap later . . . out front Hakkinen was in a class of his own, setting a new lap record as he went on to his 11th Formula 3 victory of the season, his margin 5.3 seconds over Schumacher, who was troubled by a slow puncture towards the end.'

Bennetts says that 'those foreign races he was really delighted to have won. Going back from Hockenheim to Frankfurt Airport the next day, we had two hire cars – Opels or whatever – but medium-size cars. Of course, both cars being the same we were *pushing* each other down the autobahn at whatever speed it was, 170kph, 180kph – 120-odd mph. He was driving one, I was driving the other one. He'd come up behind me, get the slipstream, push me, then I'd get past him and give him a nudge. He really was delighted.'

In the background Formula 1 teams were stirring, notably Lotus and Benetton. The latter gave him a test at Silverstone. 'The first time in a Formula 1 car, the Benetton, I wasn't nervous at all. I was confident. A big jump from Formula 3 missing out Formula 3000? No. I was finally in a proper racing car. Finally I was in the racing car that was *ultimately* quick. Finally I was in the racing car that handled like a *really* quick car – you know, like a real fast car. You had to have fast reactions, you had to brake late, you had to turn into the corners late. All these elements were there and they were what I wanted, what I *needed*. It was *absolutely* something I had dreamed about for so long, and it just came true. I wanted to go flat out, I wanted to go *so quick that nobody had ever gone quicker!*

'I don't truly know if I did do it quicker than anybody had ever done it, but I tell you one thing: I went quick enough to scare the mechanics. It was some occasion. It was the South Circuit at Silverstone, so you had a straight coming towards the pits and then a really fast right-hander. The pits are at the end of that straight. When I was coming, I was coming so fast that the mechanics thought I was going to crash into the pits. The very first lap that I did I saw the mechanics running away from the pit wall. I thought *where the hell are they going?* They were really running! After that they got used to it and for me, fantastic. That's how it went: f-a-n-t-a-s-t-i-c. I had only one spin that day and I complained immediately, because the car shouldn't have done that. The team even admitted it had a problem.'

How could you be so confident it wasn't you? After all, it was your first time in a Formula 1 car.

'Because I know the car shouldn't do sudden things, things that you don't expect, unless you are driving it like you are crazy. You should always have confidence with a car that, when you are driving it, the car will not do sudden things. That Benetton inspired confidence at a very high level, but the last bit was missing.'

There is a big question. You could make a kart go really quickly, then you get into a Formula Ford 1600, quick immediately, then into a Formula 3 car, quick immediately even though you had a bad day and went off, then into a Formula 1 car, quick immediately. You don't even seem to have to adjust, you can just do it. How?

'I think it is like this: some people have very nice handwriting and some people don't. Even if they practice like hell, the people who don't simply cannot make theirs like people who have naturally nice handwriting. Why? It's just like that, it's exactly like that.'

Are you fully aware of the fact that you can just do this and how you can do it? And that's not a silly question.

'Yes. When I am in a racing car, when I am in a road car, I know exactly what it can and will do on the edge – on the limit, if you like – every corner. That's like the handwriting.'

Every corner, even the road car?

'Anything. Either it comes naturally when you are a kid or it comes from practice. If you were to practice writing, and only writing, from five years old, then maybe 20 years later your handwriting would be fantastic, maybe not – but at least somebody gave you the chance to do it. Most people don't ever get that chance.'

Benetton were searching for a Number 2 driver to partner Nelson Piquet, and one report suggested that they were considering Roberto Moreno, Aguri Suzuki, Michael Andretti, Al Unser Jr, Ivan Capelli, Pierluigi Martini, Stefano Modena and Hakkinen, and that 'team members have made approaches to several of these drivers'. Moreno was favourite and in fact got the drive.

Lotus were poised to make their move, again in the background. And did.

A competitor in 1990 who had been and would remain a competitor, Mika Salo (giving Ukyo Katayama the birthday cake treatment at Tyrrell years later) (ICN U.K. Bureau).

Meanwhile, at the end of the season West Surrey Racing went to Macau for the Grand Prix there. Untypically, Bennetts says, 'Don't remind me of it. Macau should have been a clean sweep because it was all there for the taking. Pole no problem from Schumacher, won the first heat no problem from Schumacher [but Schumacher closed up to 2.66 seconds as they crossed the line]. In that first heat Mika had pulled out some big lead because I'd sat him down and explained to him *you understand, Mika, a two-heat race, aggregate time*, and he'd said *yes, yeah, yeah*. I said *the best thing is to drive as hard as you can in heat one safely and create as big a gap as you can so that you have it up your sleeve for heat two.* He said *yeah, yeah, I understand.*

'Mika had done a good job in heat one, took off in the lead, opened up a gap of 4.9 seconds half way through, he'd just done the quickest lap, then the lead came down.' At this point Bennetts consults a ledger (he keeps one for each of his drivers each season and they are extremely detailed). '4.8, 4.4, 4.2, 3.8, 2.9, and he crossed the line at 2.66 seconds. I asked *why didn't you stay at 4.9?* He said *Ah, it's a big lead, it's no problem.* He just shrugged his shoulders – *2.7 seconds is a long way.* I said *yes, but we had virtually 5.0 seconds.*

'For heat two we didn't change much – the brake pads, put on the third set of tyres. Mika made a bad start, Schumacher got ahead, then Mika faced the pressures you face to stay within 2.7 on aggregate. He was P2, stayed there, stayed there, he was hovering, he was closer, 0.6 of a second, then 0.4, 0.4, 0.7, 0.6, 0.5, 0.4, 0.3, 0.2, 0.3, 0.5 on lap 13 of the 15, then . . .'

Autosport reported that 'Hakkinen was closer than ever before to Schumacher's gearbox as they rounded the right-hand kink past the pits. Then he pulled out to the right to jink past Schumacher, but Schumacher moved right a fraction to block him. Hakkinen clipped the rear of the Reynard, his Ralt then spearing left into the barrier and spinning across the track to retirement. A cry of shock rendered the air. No one could believe what they had just witnessed. Hakkinen hopped from his car, then hurled his gloves at the ground in a display of titanic despair. Quite simply, he had cocked up.

'People will always wonder whether he made the bid simply in an attempt to come home with a win in both heats, to equal Senna's tally of 13 F3 wins in a season, or just because he doesn't ever like crossing

Hakkinen power at Oulton (Ian Simpson).

the line second, but they will always remember how he gave the event to Schumacher.'

Bennetts remains insistent that 'Mika just didn't need to overtake Schumacher. As long as he stayed within 2.7 he would have won, but then he started closing up, sitting 0.2 of a second behind Schumacher. We didn't have a radio in those days. If we had, I would have shouted *back off, just back off, just stay within 3 seconds.* I found out later that he had already been in heavy conversation with Lotus and he wanted to win both heats to impress. The overall victory in the Macau Grand Prix was there for the taking, but he wanted to win both heats. Mika didn't come and speak to me after the race. He disappeared. He came back a couple of hours later. I spoke to Schumacher on the Monday and he said *of course I wasn't going to make it easy for him.*'

(Suzanne Radbone offers an intriguing anecdote of her own about this. 'I think it was the evening that Mika was told he had the Lotus drive, because I remember him being quite unaffected by the accident. It didn't bother him at all. I think at that point he had been told by Keke that he had the Lotus drive.')

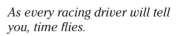

As every racing driver will tell you, time flies.

(Hakkinen family)

(Zooom, courtesy Vauxhall)

(Pascal Rondeau/Allsport)

(Photo Wilhelm, courtesy
Mercedes-Benz)

So what did happen? Hakkinen said at the time, 'I thought I was going to die. It is the worst crash I have had at speed. I closed my eyes and gripped the steering wheel when I knew I was going to hit the wall. I am disappointed with what he [Schumacher] did. It is shocking to do a thing like that when you are going at nearly 150mph. I was very surprised when he changed the line. I knew I had an excellent chance to pass, but he moved inside me.'

Schumacher said, 'I think he was crazy to try and overtake me. Nobody who has the race in his grasp should do that. It was stupid to take that risk.'

Second place would have won me the Grand Prix, but that's not how a young man thinks

These many years later, and reflecting on it, Hakkinen says, 'That was a good race. Everybody enjoyed it except Dick Bennetts, of course, because he had a lot of pride and a lot of money involved. The first heat I had pole position 1 second quicker than anybody else. Good. I felt confident. I got the lead and I won by 4, 5 seconds [Alas, no! If only he had . . .] In the second heat Schumacher took the lead and I was following him all race long just hanging in there. That was all I had to do: follow him home.

'After the start-finish line there was a very fast right-hand corner where you went fifth gear flat out, like 230kph [the 150mph, give or take]. That car with the downforce it had was mega-quick. Schumacher went wide. Unusual. You don't go wide through there. Anyway, he went wide and he slowed down a lot. I was coming like a rocket so I decided to overtake him in a straight line [after the corner]. Easy. The moment that I tried to overtake him he changed his line and we touched and I lost my front wing and I crashed.

'Naturally mega-disappointment, everybody was disappointed, the mechanics, everybody, but at the end of the day it was a racing accident. I mean, things like that shouldn't happen, but they do happen. Of course I wanted to win the race. Of course second place would have won me the Grand Prix, but that's not how a young man thinks. Yes, Dick was annoyed, yes he was. I repeat that Macau was disappointing, really disappointing, but I'm afraid that that is motor racing. You cannot always win. Sometimes you lose. Sometimes you make a mistake. Sometimes you take a chance you shouldn't have taken. It is exactly like that.

'So we lost that day by bad luck, but we had great victories during the year, too. We won the Championship, we won the Imola race, we won the Hockenheim race: a great season. I know Dick was upset because if we'd won Macau and added Fuji it meant a lot of money, but I didn't think that way. The money was not important.'

Bennetts remembers that 'because the car had been shunted so badly, it screwed up Fuji as well. In those days there was a £20,000 bonus if you won both races, and as far as I was concerned we had a £10,000 bill for a damaged car, too. In total it cost us £30,000. We had to build a new car and it had to be worked on until 1 o'clock in the morning in the Macau garage [on the Sunday]. We had a spare tub with us, brand new, never been used. The last we saw of the car was 1 o'clock, 2 o'clock Monday morning at Macau. Then it had to go from Macau to Hong Kong by boat, be flown to Tokyo, then taken by road from Tokyo to Fuji. We didn't set eyes on the car again until Thursday morning at Fuji, and it wasn't just the building of a new car: we had Marlboro livery on it for Macau, but Casio at Fuji, which meant a change from red and white to blue and white. Five little Japanese guys were working on our two cars all through the night changing all the fablon to Casio livery. We did an all-nighter on it to make it ready for the Friday at Fuji.

'Of course it was raining on the Friday – first practice day – and Mika couldn't quite diagnose the circuit because it was his first time at Fuji. It was difficult for him to know, plus we'd had to rush and build the car in a hurry, plus we'd had little mechanical problems. One was something underneath, so you couldn't see it, plus the guys had done the all-nighter and they were knackered. It was a disaster.'

Mika Hakkinen did not qualify for the Fuji Grand Prix, which Schumacher won. That did not disturb the overall perception that Hakkinen was good – good enough.

• CHAPTER FOUR •

The
power game

DOUBTS HAD BEEN gathering over the future of Lotus. Peter Collins was known to be seeking finance urgently while rumours circulated that various people might buy it. Lotus survived under Collins and were soon working hard to have their new car ready; and Collins did sign Hakkinen.

'I'd been at Silverstone in 1990 watching the Formula 3 race,' Collins says, 'and I saw the dice going on between Salo and Hakkinen for the lead. From what I'd seen I rated both of them, and that came in handy much later on, too, when we took Salo for the Japanese Grand Prix of 1994. [Lotus suddenly needed a replacement for their Belgian driver Philippe Adams who had bought his way into the last two Grands Prix but hadn't paid up yet.]

'In 1990 I didn't basically know either of the Mikas. I knew of Mika Hakkinen a tiny bit because I'd met him once or twice with Keke and, of course, I knew Keke well. I'm not sure if Mika knew who I was – well, he may have done, but he didn't know me as someone to walk up and talk to. When we decided to go ahead with Lotus, I looked at the potentially available Formula 1 drivers around at the time and none of them particularly motivated or inspired me.'

Collins rang Bennetts. 'Peter asked me about Mika,' Bennetts recounts. 'I said *natural talent, promotable, a good easy-going guy*. I was pleased for Mika to get into Formula 1. We'd love to have kept him another year, but once a young driver has won the Formula 3 Championship what has he to gain by staying? Possibly we should have been a bit tighter on him [in the sense of discipline/control/pushing], but being supported by Marlboro and managed by Rosberg I assumed that all that should have been done.'

Collins rang Rosberg. 'I'm going to make an attempt to keep Team Lotus running. What about moving Mika into Formula 1 next year?'

Rosberg: 'You can't be serious.' The usual route was to go into Formula 3000 after Formula 3, not vault directly into Formula 1.

Collins: 'Yes, I am.'

Rosberg: 'How much money would you need?'

Collins told him and Rosberg thought that wouldn't be a problem. This matter of money can baffle outsiders to motor sport as much as team orders do. Put simply, a young driver must expect to bring money to a team in order to secure a drive with them, and there are those who only remain in Formula 1 because they bring money. Once a driver graduates to a leading team, however, he can expect to be paid, and in millions.

Collins, in charge of a team with a desperate need for finance, had struck a balance. 'For me it was the ideal situation. I thought the guy had tremendous talent and potential and personal sponsorship. Yes, ideal, and that's why we signed him.'

In other words, he was a real driver rather than just a pay driver?

'He paid to drive, but he was a "real" driver, oh yes. We took him principally on talent, but obviously being able to bring sponsorship made it possible for us to give him a season. I mean, he didn't pay for his whole season by any means, and in the eyes of a lot of people it was still a fairly adventurous thing to do to pluck the guy straight out of Formula 3. I didn't really have any doubts from the day we signed him.'

That was in December 1990. 'I can't really take it in at the moment,' Hakkinen said. 'I'm still upside-down. It's very difficult for me to explain because I am so surprised by it. Keke only told me last night. I thought *Jeez, this is really great.* I'm so grateful to Keke – he's done an excellent job.'

Hakkinen tested a Lotus at Silverstone in late January doing 40 laps and setting a best time of 1m 30.70s. 'I was just getting miles, going round and round running myself in and getting used to the grip, downforce, brakes and tyres. We didn't try anything new,' he said at the time.

Collins expands on having 'absolutely no doubts' about signing Hakkinen. 'It was after the second lap I saw Mika do in the Formula 1 car at the Silverstone test. We took one of the 1989 cars with the Judd engine just to get him acclimatised to Formula 1 power. He wasn't at all worried about it, wasn't nervous – he was quite looking forward to it. We ran through the briefing, the instruments, how to drive it, etc, etc, and he went out and did an installation lap, came in. *Everything all right?* we asked. *Yep,* he said.

'I was going to go out and watch somewhere on the circuit. I went down to Club [the right-hander out at the back of the circuit] and first lap through, OK, he was reasonably slow, just sort of finding his way. Second lap through he was on the power, fully confident, just *into it*. He came round again obviously enjoying himself immensely, and that was it. I got in my car, drove to the pits, said goodbye to everybody and went back to the factory with a smile on my face. He was going to be a star.'

Hakkinen insists that 'again it was a normal thing as it had been with Benetton. This was another Formula 1 car but the same dream – and again exactly what I had been dreaming, the sort of car I wanted: speed, reactions, everything. Peter mentions the second lap, but for me it wouldn't matter if it was the third or fourth or whatever.'

Hakkinen means that he could handle the car no problem, wasn't surprised to be on the pace straight away and, overall, you could have picked any lap. It is the same with all the naturally fast men: not that they are capable of constructing a single hot lap, but that they can do it again and again – and again. And what's the fuss?

Hakkinen moved to Wymondham, which was the nearest place to the Lotus factory. Thereby hangs a tale of Suzanne Radbone. 'I had met PC [Peter Collins] at Adelaide. Mika was leaving West Surrey. I contacted PC and I went to see him. He was starting the fledgling re-born Lotus, he saw a fellow Aussie in me – I think – and thought, *well if we need anybody we need Suzanne,* so a bit by chance I arrived a couple of days before Mika. I found a four-bedroomed house in Wymondham, big living area and all that sort of thing.'

Initially it was just going to be for Radbone and another member of the Lotus team. 'I described it to Mika and gave him directions and said to him *if you want to pop up at any time you can stay,* etc. He arrived one Sunday evening with his car full of his gear, so I presumed he was moving in. That was Mika, very casual about things like that.'

I tackled Hakkinen on this delightful story and although he can't remember the details he was sure he *had* discussed it with Suzanne and put on his best *believe me* voice when he said it. Mind you, he was smiling broadly when he told me that . . .

Who would partner Hakkinen at Lotus? Rumours circulated that Martin Donnelly, badly injured in Spain in 1990, might well as soon as he was fit, Johnny Herbert deputising until then. Other rumours spoke of the German Bernd Schneider, who'd done a couple of seasons with Zakspeed, then, in 1990, a couple of races with Footwork Arrows.

In February, Briton Julian Bailey moved into contention when, at Collins's request, he tested the new Lotus at Silverstone. Herbert, the usual Lotus test driver, wasn't available and Collins said, 'We wanted someone with experience in the new car while Mika Hakkinen got more mileage in the old one.' A week later, Bailey was announced as the team's Number 1 driver on the understanding that he held the position only until Donnelly returned.

Bailey and Hakkinen went to Phoenix for the United States Grand Prix, the first race of the season. Bailey failed to qualify but Hakkinen

Peter Collins (right) shakes hands with sponsorship-finder Guy Edwards in the Lotus days.

did, in mid-grid. One report (*Motoring News*) said, 'The rookie Finn proved the sensation of practice, adapting to Formula 1 with barely a flicker of emotion. To watch him out on the track was to see a young driver totally at ease with an unfamiliar situation, and how easy it was to forget that he had no experience of qualifying tyres.'

In the Friday morning free practice, Hakkinen began his Formula 1 career with an exploratory lap of 1m 54.012s and circled for another six laps, when he did a 1m 32.616. He made a total of four runs, with the final lap a 1m 28.394. First qualifying was instructive, too: 28 laps in seven runs, working down from an opening 1m 48.569 to 1m 27.320, 22nd quickest of the 30 entries and beating the Ligiers (Thierry Boutsen and Eric Comas), the Footworks (Michele Alboreto and Alex Caffi), the AGS of Stefan Johansson, Mark Blundell (Brabham), team-mate Bailey, and Ivan Capelli (Leyton House).

I don't want to make too much of this, particularly since it is 'only' a qualifying session, but it does demonstrate how soon Hakkinen became comfortable within a competitive Formula 1 context and at a street circuit with, by definition, no room for error or much experimentation. Second qualifying confirmed everything, emphasising how a natural driver learns and adapts almost simultaneously to it happening. The sequence

First run	2m 27.711, warming up to
	1m 27.328
Second run	1m 54.588, warming up to
	1m 25.448

at which point he had to hand the car over to Bailey, whose own was suffering from mechanical problems. 'I'm surprised to qualify so high,' Hakkinen said. 'I did have two spins in second-gear corners where I was lucky not to hit the wall, but I like street circuits. I was disappointed on Friday, and before I came here maybe I'd tended to be sceptical when I heard people in Formula 1 talking all the time about traffic, but it is the truth. It can be very bad!'

Motoring News concluded that 'his driving position looked desperately uncomfortable as he hunched forward in a crouch, but nothing stopped him from making a very impressive debut, which historians will doubtless look back on fondly as his career progresses.'

And I have, and I have . . .

'He just has natural talent and a natural feel for it,' Collins says. 'He doesn't have to think about how quick he goes. And guys like Mika can do it in anything and with anything. If you gave Mika a gun to shoot, even if he'd never shot a gun in his life, he'd do it well because he has good hand-eye co-ordination. That's what makes a good driver.'

The 1m 25.448 compared to Senna's pole of 1m 21.434, a huge difference of course, but that misses the point. Hakkinen was on his way.

The race provided a rude introduction to the stresses and dangers of Formula 1. On lap 8 he hit a bump and his knee struck the steering wheel release mechanism. Flat out in fifth down the back straight the wheel began to work loose. 'That was scary, you know. We had taken some padding off the dashboard, but when a bump jogged my knee against what was left, somehow it affected the quick release. I couldn't believe my eyes! The car was pulling to the right and I was fumbling with my left hand trying to clamp the steering wheel back while braking very hard. My heart was going barp, barp, barp.'

It wasn't that he didn't have any money, it was that he didn't think in those terms

---

He pitted, dropping him from 16th to last, and sat out a long stop while the problem was properly investigated. 'I mean, I just couldn't trust it not to do the same again. The corner on to Washington Street is flat in fourth. You go off there and it's hospital, definitely.' He ran to lap 59 when the engine failed, and, before he left for the airport, insisted that he'd have qualified 1.5 seconds faster if he had had more experience of the special tyres.

He put the Lotus on the third last row of the grid in Brazil, but the instant he'd done that, mid-way through the second session, he had to hand the car to Bailey whose own suffered a small fire; again Lotus lacked a spare. Bailey didn't qualify for the race. Hakkinen kept on and finished ninth three laps behind the winner, Senna.

Reflecting on these two races, Hakkinen said insistently, 'No, I had no problem adjusting to the car. The biggest thing in Formula 1 is the bloody speed. It is so fast and sometimes it is difficult to concentrate on the car because you are concentrating on yourself. That is the first thing you learn. The rest is done automatically: you brake later and if you go a little bit wide it helps you find the limit. You can find that out the first time you do a Formula 1 test, but you don't do it at 300kph, you do it at 100kph!' Remember what Peter Collins said about Hakkinen's very first lap at Silverstone.

'My strategy was to take it carefully at the start in Brazil. I very much wanted to know what it was like to drive a full Grand Prix distance. The car and the engine ran well and I could have run quicker for longer, but it was hard. We are still struggling with the seat fitting a bit and my back muscles get really tense. I did a lot of training before I started the season, but I still need to do more. The forces are unbelievable. People cannot even imagine what it is like. It's crazy. You go through the corner and you can't hold your head. It is something that you cannot explain because you cannot imagine what it is like until you do it. Then you understand . . .'

Hakkinen and Bailey qualified for the San Marino Grand Prix at Imola, albeit on the last row of the grid. Bailey says, 'The situation was that things in Formula 1 never did work out for me apart from Imola, where I should have beaten Mika. I was a lot quicker than him in the race, but I constantly kept getting stuck in neutral so that every time I passed him – and I was quicker than him, you know – I'd get stuck in neutral and he'd come past again! He wasn't terribly quick in the race. He was good in qualifying, but in the race he was still playing himself in to Formula 1, so to speak. He was taking that sort of approach, getting miles under his belt, but there is no doubt that at Imola I was quicker than him in the wet [Bailey out-qualified Hakkinen on the Saturday when it was wet] and in the dry in the race.' Hakkinen finished fifth, Bailey sixth, but both three laps behind the winner, Senna.

'So then at Monaco he was a lot quicker than me, so, er . . .'

Hakkinen was on the last row of the grid again, but Bailey did not qualify and his Grand Prix career ended. 'There was certainly never any friction between us,' Bailey says. 'If our partnership had gone on there might have been. It depends on who has the upper hand. You've got to remember that he had Rosberg behind him as well, and I think he was paying something like a million dollars to drive for the Lotus team, whereas I hadn't paid anything, really. I was supposed to pay, but I never actually came up with the money. Peter Collins then took

Johnny Herbert on board. The thing was, I had signed a contract and Collins never actually took me to court, which was quite decent of him really. Not that I had anything, anyway, that he could have had [chuckle]. He would have been wasting *his* money trying to get money from me. I didn't have any.

'Although I was his first team-mate in Formula 1, I didn't know him at all before that [they'd been in the Macau Grand Prix in 1989, but so had plenty of others; Bailey was seven years older, more senior and had had no reason to speak to the chubby-faced blond youngster]. I just sort of met him up at Lotus. He had already signed, anyway, before I got there. He was a part of the team. I don't really know him that well even now, to be honest.

Hakkinen's Grand Prix debut at Phoenix, 1991 (Pascal Rondeau/Allsport).

'When he first came to Formula 1 he was the sort of guy who never had any money in his pocket. You'd get to the airport with him and he wouldn't have arranged a hire car. He always expected everything to be done for him at that stage. I think he had always been cosseted: like when we got to a toll on the motorway he never had any money to pay for it. He always expected someone else to have it, you know. It wasn't that he didn't have any money, it was that he didn't think in those terms. I thought he was very immature to start with, because of things like that. I remember driving with him to Imola and I said *right, I'll drive, I'll pay for the car, I'll pay for the tolls, all you've got to do is read the map*, and when we come to a junction where we had to make a decision whether to go left or right he was fast asleep! That's the sort of thing that used to brass me off, because he expected everything to be done for him.

The poll tax and electricity bills and phone bills were just not part of his agenda

---

'He was very young and he's not like that now, he's a totally different person, because Formula 1 has turned him into a man. In those days he'd just come out of Formula 3, hadn't he? I got the impression that everything had been taken care of until then and, of course, Peter Collins was taking care of him, too, by entrusting him to me: namely, I'm going to Imola and he's going to come with me, and I'm going to get there and I'm going to get him there, and he's going to go to sleep [chuckle].' On the track, however, Bailey was 'impressed with Hakkinen's qualifying straight away.'

I'm curious about the difference between doing a qualifying lap and doing it repetitively in the race. 'I don't know because I've never had any difference, really,' Bailey says. 'For me a qualifying lap and a race lap are the same, which is why I haven't qualified that well sometimes [chuckle]. That's a fact for me. The only thing that makes a difference is that you get more grip on new tyres. I think Hakkinen can stretch himself in qualifying sometimes . . .'

Incidentally, the notion of everything being taken care of demands exploration because it is not a feeling every driver has known. I asked McNish to reflect on what Bailey has just said.

'It's a reasonably fair comment that things had been done for Mika – and myself – in a lot of ways to try and help our careers. There were things that were taken care of the further you went. And, you know, Julian had been in the business longer than Mika [so maybe it was natural for him to look after his younger team-mate]. I am sure Mika can hire his own car now [chuckle]. You also have to remember that Mika had Keke helping him right from the start, and there'd been JJ Lehto with his successes, and Mika followed on from those successes, which meant that it was a little bit easier for Mika to make it than most.'

Another lady, Anita Smith, 'got involved because Suzanne was a friend of mine. When Mika went to Lotus she went with him as a racing secretary, but it was purely platonic – oh yes, absolutely – none of that naughty business. They were just really good friends. I met Suzanne because I was working in Formula 3 in 1989, she was working for Dick and we were the only girls, really. We got together and when she went to Lotus I stayed in touch with her. I used to go up and spend a lot of time there. It was a lovely, rambling, huge house at Wymondham, a really, really nice big house that Suzanne found and did everything for. Mika was a lazy bugger! He absolutely had a heart of gold when he could be bothered not to be selfish – well, he wasn't selfish in a nasty way, bless him, but in a thoughtless way. You know, when someone doesn't mean to be horrible at all and if they ever thought they were being horrible they'd feel mortified . . .

'He didn't seem to have a care in the world, certainly financially. I imagine that he wasn't too strapped for cash. Suze would pay the rent on the house – which was £550 or whatever – and the phone bill and the gas bill, and there would always be food in the fridge, and milk and bread and so on. It was all taken care of. I just remember Mika being swept along by everything, no real comprehension that Suzanne was earning £11,000 a year or whatever. I do know that it wasn't a great deal.

'If she said *Ah, Mika, you owe me £700 in rent* she'd get a cheque straight away. *Oh my God, Suzanne, I am so sorry, Suzanne.* He genuinely was sorry. He was not being a cad or trying to get out of paying. He had one interest and it was racing cars. Suzanne did take over the role of mother very obviously, and Keke Rosberg used to say that without Suzanne he didn't know what Mika would have done –

because he was completely incapable of going to the shop and buying a newspaper!'

Suzanne Radbone confirms this. 'The poll tax and electricity bills and phone bills were just not part of his agenda. Not interested.'

I point out to Radbone that Anita Smith said that she was paying the bills and that Hakkinen wasn't being mean, he just didn't think about these things, and when she mentioned them he paid instantly.

'He was renowned for being tight at Lotus,' Radbone replied. 'He never had any money on him. There is a story that he went testing with a group of guys at a place called, I think, Black Rock in the States. It was a Goodyear proving ground. They all went for a drink after testing and Mika said *I'll buy everyone a drink* and turned to his chief mechanic and said *can I borrow 20 dollars to pay for them?* That was standard Mika. He just never had any money on him. Initially I gave him the benefit of the doubt: possibly he was given an allowance by Keke to live on, and because he comes from a very middle-of-the-road family – charming people – he really didn't have any grasp. He had always been looked after by his parents and then by Keke. Booking an hotel, for example, never crossed his mind.'

But it must *have crossed his mind.*

A wet test session at Silverstone (both Ian Simpson).

'I'll have to give him the benefit of the doubt [chuckle] and say it was naivety, but as time went on it was that he was tight. Things like the phone bill, just silly things he couldn't understand. Why on earth would somebody have to pay a TV licence? You buy a TV and that's it, no discussion, end of story.

'So we finished up living in this house. PC moved in with his wife Jane and daughter Sam for a while, and also Nigel Stepney [a Lotus mechanic]. We were quite full. That was the sort of environment Mika enjoyed. He liked to have people around him. He is not the sort of person to be on his own very much. He enjoyed the family atmosphere of it all, I suppose, and the fact that he was being taken care of. We organised a gym for him to go to in Norwich and he finished up having one of the trainers at the gym becoming his personal trainer and not paying him a penny! This chap would arrive at the house and wake him up in the morning, have breakfast with him and they'd go for a run and work-out – so Mika had it well sussed. There is a way about Mika that is quite innocent – well, it comes across as quite innocent, as quite completely hopeless.' (Again natural justice demands that Hakkinen be given the right of reply, which can be summarised as follows: *I did pay the trainer!*)

I can't believe he was as innocent as he made out because he was a young boy away from home

The choirboy syndrome? 'Exactly. Mika was an obvious talent. A lot of the things that went on were very minor in the grand scheme of things, weren't really important, but that didn't make him a choirboy – although he gave that choirboy impression, always did. I do think, incidentally, that time will prove that he is an exceptional talent on natural ability.'

I mention how Dick Bennetts recounts tales of Hakkinen night-clubbing with Christian Fittipaldi, and next morning Fittipaldi complaining of a hangover and Hakkinen insisting he hadn't drunk much. 'He was believable to a certain degree. I can't believe he was as innocent as he made out, because he was a young boy away from home. In coming across as naive it showed that he was more sophisticated' – in being able to appear naive!

But Fittipaldi admitted he'd been drinking heavily . . .

'. . . whereas Mika never would. He never would right through his Lotus days. He would never concede any point when it came to his behaviour or anything like that.'

With a woman's intuition, what did you make of this?

'The innocence started out as Mika's way of coping because he wasn't quite sure how he would be accepted as the person who really was a night-clubber. He was very keen on young ladies, to the point of usually driving down the street and pointing one out. His standard line was *Oh my God* in his very heavy Finnish accent. Anything in a skirt, really, would draw his eye, and in that respect he was entirely normal. Yet he would try and be this angel in his bosses' eyes. Mind you, there weren't lots of women ringing the house or anything like that, although Mika did have a mobile phone that was constantly glued to his ear, so . . .'

What did you make of these two simultaneous Hakkinens, the choirboy and the virile man-about-town? 'I imagined that Mika had life pretty well sussed, that he was going places, he was young, he was cute, and he had a belief in his own ability. In a way, I suppose, I expected that one day the two would meet and he'd become a more normal adult – it was an abnormal existence for him, anyway. I thought that one day he'd break out but he never really did. Then he moved to Monaco and whatever he did was private from the team. He could be himself, which I think he probably needed to be. He *is* very charming and in a childlike way, I suppose, a choirboy. To all intents and purposes, yes, a choirboy. He led a charmed existence. I don't think he'd intentionally hurt anybody. I didn't see any young ladies with bleeding hearts pounding on the door or anything like that.'

And again natural justice demands that Hakkinen be given a full opportunity. I reproduce his response verbatim, complete with accompanying noises and facial expressions.

Suzanne told me stories which I found surprising: that you seemed more innocent than you really were. You know what a choirboy is? A little boy who wears white and sings in church?

'Ah!'

She said you could be like a choirboy but you weren't.

[Erupts in wild laughter] 'Oh, Jesus. [Raises voice] How does she know?'

Woman's intuition.

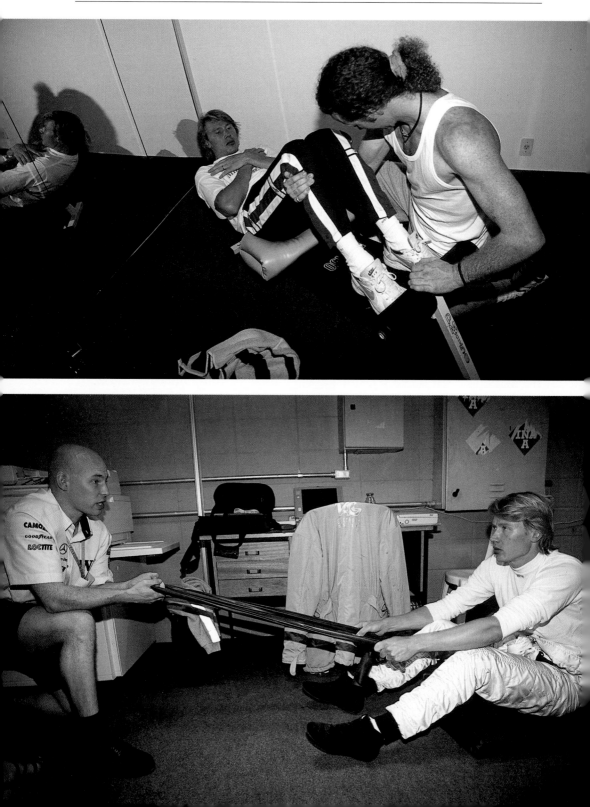

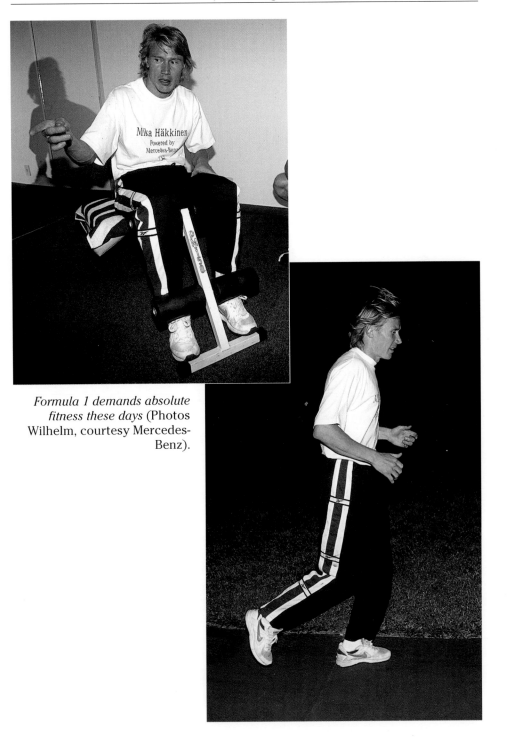

Formula 1 demands absolute fitness these days (Photos Wilhelm, courtesy Mercedes-Benz).

'All right. [Chuckles, pauses] Do you want me to say something about this?'

Yes.

'I-am-very-innocent. [Face cracks into all-consuming, naughty urchin grin]

Not what she thought.

[Erupts in wild laughter again] 'What did she say, what did she say?'

That you were clever.

[Rumbling laughter] 'Does she have proof I wasn't innocent? I don't know – like I say, I was really laid back and maybe she means that. I was a person who didn't take too much stress about things. Maybe she means I was innocent like that.'

Also you didn't create any problems.

'No, I didn't.'

It was just that you didn't do anything much at all except sit and be happy.

'Yeah. Mind you, Suzanne didn't know me that well. She knew me, but she didn't know me that well.'

Normally a Formula 1 driver is hyper-active, on top of everything . . .

'. . . but all people are individuals. We are all different. Some people have a talent to drive the car, but other aspects of their lives can be different. I don't think I am a laid-back person. It just looks like that, maybe because I am very relaxed. I don't take panic out of things.' [An utterly delightful way of saying *I don't panic*. Sometimes non-English speakers enrich the English language by wielding the words as they do, and sometimes use the language as a shield – hence, maybe, the smoke screen surrounding being laid-back, not being laid-back, and mistaking all that for being relaxed. Clever . . .]

One of the themes of this book is that you always seem to find people to look after you.

'Hmmm. No, not really. That's not correct. That's history maybe, that's in the past. Of course there have been certain times in my life when . . . well, let me give you an example. In 1988 I jumped into my car, I'd packed all my stuff in that car – all my clothes – and I drove it on to a shipping boat – or what do you call it? – a cargo boat in Helsinki and I take this boat to England, four days' trip, day and night, day and night. This was when I got the deal with Dragon Motorsport and I was going to England to race. When I get to England the whole world is open for me. So I'm driving out of this cargo boat at

Felixstowe, 4 o'clock in the morning. Automatically you think *shall I go left or shall I go right? Where shall I go?* You have no idea. So of course you rely on a lot of people helping.

'We have all known this feeling where you arrive somewhere strange and think *what do I do now?* Automatically you need people who are organising your life to a certain extent. You need that element. You need what I call Management. This office [Rosberg's office in Monte Carlo, April 1997, Jatta in one room and Didier Coton in another, organising, defining, ultimately protecting] does things for me. To a certain extent you need this. Otherwise you get mad. You cannot do it all yourself. You get tired. You get fed up. You cannot do all the things, cannot travel, cope with the Press work, and *that* and *that* and *that*. Cannot. These days you can give a certain amount of your time but not more. You need help. I rely on these people a lot. They look after me.'

If people are willing to help me or are attracted to me, I cannot answer it – I don't know why

---

When you were young you were looked after.
'Absolutely. Of course.'
People were very protective of you.
'Yes, that's correct.'
And they didn't know why, and you were there like a choirboy, smiling.
[Chuckle] 'Yeah, I don't know why either!'
This is not the sort of thing I could be discussing with almost any other Formula 1 driver because frankly it wouldn't be possible.
'Hmmm. I cannot answer that myself. If people are willing to help me or are attracted to me – I don't mean sexually, I mean the other way – I cannot answer it. I don't know why.'
Have you been conscious of this, people wanting to mother you, even the men.
[Eruption of laughter cascading in ripples round the room] 'Oh dear. [Voice lost in the laughter. When it subsides:] That's a good one. [Long reflective pause]. 'I have a feeling it's not that innocent smile, that blond hair – maybe that has got something to do with it, also – but it's a lot to do with the personality, what a person is like. I can be an arrogant bastard if I want, but this is not my personality. That would be

pretending. I grew up with manners. I learned with the help of my parents, with the help of my schooling, with the help of the style of living in Finland, that these good manners are a part of everyday life. I like that. Also, the talent to drive the car very fast must have an effect.'

Namely you're famous, and fame itself is an attraction. I recount that in an earlier book by PSL on Johnny Herbert – The Steel behind the Smile – fellow driver Perry McCarthy described how his (McCarthy's) father felt a need to look after/protect Herbert but didn't feel the same need to protect Perry, his own son.

'. . . maybe because Johnny had a talent.'

Maybe. Herbert was into the choirboy syndrome, too. Never mind.

The Lotus of 1992, here testing at Silverstone (Ian Simpson).

'It's a lot about what kind of education you have in your life. There are not so many nice people any more. [Talking fast] It's a tough world – it is tough, it's hard, it's a tough world. We are in a hard business. I think people like other people who still have feelings, a warm heart, people who can smile and be happy. Even if there is a hard life going on around you, people like that.'

Alcorn, the Formula 3 opponent, pays a nice tribute. 'When Mika went into Formula 1, I was out of racing by then and into television. We were doing a lot of work with Lotus, who, of course, Mika had just joined. I spent time around Lotus – he was one of the drivers I respected, anyway.'

Why?

'He was a good driver and out there on the track it was a battle to

overtake him. He knew how to drive, he knew how to overtake . . .'

To summarise this first season of Formula 1, after Monaco Hakkinen spun off in Canada, was ninth in Mexico, did not qualify in France, was 12th in Britain, the engine failed in Germany, was 14th in Hungary, the engine failed in Belgium, was 14th in Italy and Portugal and spun off in Spain and Japan. That left Australia.

Radbone remembers that 'he stayed with friends of mine here in Melbourne because he didn't have a holiday destination that he wanted to go to [between the Japanese and Australian races] and he had nobody to go with. He stayed in the spare room at a friend's place. It was almost as if *Suzanne's going on holiday to Melbourne, oh, Mika must be going, yeah, yeah, he is.* It was just this assumption that this little lap dog – no, lap dog's the wrong word – just this assumption that he would follow me. It was never the situation that he would help me out or get me organised or carry my bags – it was never anything like that, never crossed his mind. He was late coming down from Japan because I think he had to stay on and do various promotional activities in Tokyo. Then he took a flight. He didn't ring me or tell me when he was coming; he jumped on the plane, arrived in Melbourne and sat on his suitcase in Arrivals expecting me to be there!'

What happened outside of a racing car was of really secondary importance

I'm curious about how is it possible for a man to drive a Formula 1 car, which involves a terrific awareness of all manner of factors, then fly to Australia and not be aware he hasn't told someone so they could meet him.

'What happened outside of a racing car was of really secondary importance,' Radbone says. 'His natural ability got him that far, got him as far as a drive in a Formula 1 car – which requires a tremendous amount of ability. It wasn't a bought drive or anything like that.

'He was never afraid of anything. That was the thing with Mika. He was never afraid of travelling or going out and giving it a go. For him, jumping on a plane and travelling round the world was *well, that's fine, we'll do that.* He just had this confidence in his ability. If I hadn't turned up at Melbourne Airport he'd probably have wandered along and talked to some lovely lady in a hire car place and charmed her. He was charming in a lot of ways, and that's his ability not to be bothered. A very cool sort of character in that respect. I can't live like that and, because I can't live like that, it was to Mika's benefit [chuckle] . . .'

Collins evaluates that first season. 'He did well but actually he could have done better. He was still very young at that stage and I think he almost went a little bit too well too early. I think he got a bit complacent about how easy it was, and also, in the early part of the season, he wasn't really pushed by his team-mate. It was only when Johnny came along that he actually had to work much harder. It was apparent that whenever Johnny was at a race Mika qualified better and worked harder – certainly than when, say, Michael Bartels was driving.' Bartels, a German, did Germany, Hungary, Italy and Spain for Lotus in 1991, but did not qualify for any of them.

I got the impression that Mika and Johnny were good team-mates.

'Yes, they were very good team-mates. I also think the atmosphere in the team encouraged that. There was no room for prima donnas, not anywhere in the team, and that included the drivers. They were expected to do their bit. I guess because of where we were at the time, and where we were planning to go, if necessary we'd give them a bit of a smacking – though not punching! I've had Mika by the arm a few times ripping into him because of his immaturity. It was the sort of thing you couldn't do with someone who had been around for a few years, and it wasn't bullying, it was just trying to get the message across rather than having him spending time learning at our expense, if you know what I mean. We couldn't really afford that sort of time.'

How did he take that? Did he take it all right?

'Yeah, he did. I think he was a bit gob-smacked the first time he got an earful, but I must say that we got on well through the whole period. I genuinely believed, you see, that when we signed them Mika and Johnny were going to do a better job than most of the more experienced journeymen we could have had. Mika and Johnny would be immediately quicker, and even better in the future. And, as it turned out, they *were* quicker than the journeymen and still had the potential to be better and better. For instance, we took Johnny because we believed he was under-rated and had great potential. He didn't bring a penny [in terms of paying for the drive].'

How did Hakkinen *take it?*

'Things could have been different – things can always be different – but the pressure that Collins had that year and those years was more than too much,' says Mika. 'In one sense he was not hard on me because he was just as hard on himself and he expected the same from other people. I was quite laid back and he was pushing me, *go, go, do this, do that*. In another sense he was too hard on me because I did not understand why he was doing it. I understand now when I look back, but then I was living with it every minute. I believe that before you do things in your career and your life you have to understand why you are doing them. If you don't understand why, it is a waste of time. This is not always easy for a young man, which I was.' Twenty-three, very young in Formula 1 terms.

For Hakkinen a controversial Belgian Grand Prix at Spa in 1992 – Collins was critical of the drive he put together (Pascal Rondeau/Allsport).

Some people respond to pushing; other people don't respond to that.

'I'm the person who – [long, long pause] – I'm the person who works with great motivation. If I have the right motivation I can do very good things very well indeed. It doesn't matter if it's night or day, I don't care, as long as I have the belief and the motivation. When I don't have the belief and the motivation I have no reason to do something.'

Yes, but does being pushed help the motivation?

'Not necessarily. It depends on the situation, but if I feel I am giving the maximum, driving a car very fast indeed, there is no point in coming to me and saying *you can drive faster* – because I am already doing it. The car can be better, which is a different thing altogether, so the concentration has to be on the car and people be motivated to make the car better.'

The season of 1992, the second with Lotus, represented a distinct advance in Hakkinen's career. He finished eighth in the Championship with 11 points and scored regularly in the second half of the season after being sixth in Mexico early on: fourth in France, sixth at Silverstone, fourth in Hungary, sixth in Belgium, fifth in Portugal.

'There were times,' Collins says, 'when Keke felt I was being too hard on Mika, but I think Keke wasn't fully aware of what was going on. Mika was taking it a little bit too easy, but once he got his head down and started working harder he actually did a good job, and in 1992 he drove very, very well. The team should have had a lot more results – for example, at Suzuka Johnny was running second and the gearbox failed, but, you know, those things happen. Mika's physical condition let him down a couple of times in 1992 because I don't think he put enough into conditioning himself. I've come across a lot of very talented drivers who can do things so easily that they can be a bit lazy when it comes to getting down to fitness.'

Like Ronnie Peterson and so on?

'They can be brilliantly talented drivers, but they don't really see the importance of being fit. Some drivers can be fit without looking it, like Niki Lauda who obviously was fit [but didn't look as if he could run and catch a bus]. Initially I don't think Mika trained hard enough and also I think he was a little bit psychologically weak in respect of having the mental will to go through the pain barrier. When you drive at a certain level and keep up driving at that level it takes a lot out of you.'

At this point, Collins reaches for ways to describe the tiny

The style and lifestyle of a star.

Left *A photo session for BOSS, where he was told to look serious* (BOSS).

Above With girlfriend Erja . . .

. . . *and demonstrating the art of explanation* (Photos Wilhelm, courtesy Mercedes-Benz).

Straight down the middle (Craig Prentis/Allsport).

differences that magnify themselves in Formula 1. They are almost, but not quite, contradictions.

'It wasn't difficult to drive a whole race, that wasn't the problem. How can I explain it? What it came down to was that if he got tired in a race he'd back off – not back off completely, but he wouldn't be trying *as hard*. Now it's a fact of life that in any race when you are at that level there is a threshold point that you've got to *burn* through, and initially he wasn't doing that. He was facing the threshold and letting it get the better of him. Subsequently he got on top of that and it didn't affect him then.

In any race there is a threshold point that you've got to burn through – he wasn't doing that

---

'I think Keke felt I was very biased about Johnny, but particularly at Spa [in the 1992 Belgian Grand Prix]. I had been critical of Mika because he had been extremely strong in the early laps [briefly up to fourth on lap 5] and with three or four laps to go he'd just given up and lost a place [to Senna, in fact, with two laps to go]. I believe it was an example of *well, my team mate is further back, he's not a threat, I'm OK, it'll be pretty good if I finish where I am in this car with this team, etc*. But he was young then. I am sure his attitude is different today.'

At season's end rumours circulated that Hakkinen and Riccardo Patrese were Williams's favoured choice to partner Alain Prost for 1993. Damon Hill got that drive, of course. A strange situation developed, Senna reluctant to commit himself to another season with Marlboro McLaren although in mid-January Dennis said, 'I have everything in place except my third driver.' Moreover, the test driver might be instantly promoted to race if Senna didn't sign. Hakkinen was keen, but had a contract with Lotus; it went to the Contract Recognition Board, who ruled that Lotus didn't have a binding hold over him. He joined McLaren.

About the leaving – was it messy?

'Yes, it was,' Collins says.

Do you want to talk about it?

'Not particularly. I mean, I feel it was completely inappropriate after what we had done for him – what the team had done for him – yes, very much so – and because of the agreement that had been reached. I felt pretty unhappy with that, but, you know, it's all water under the bridge now.'

I asked Hakkinen to talk about Collins. 'He had mega-pressure on him. I still today don't understand how he was able to handle it. He worked so hard. He was doing everything and it was too much for him. When I went jogging from the house in Wymondham in the evenings I'd go past the factory, might be 8 o'clock, might be cold and raining, and I'd be jogging like crazy. I'd see a little light on up there. It was Peter Collins's office and he was there working. Every night.

'When you look at the race results, we were getting points. I don't think many people respected Peter Collins enough. If he had had more support – if people had understood and respected how much he worked – we would have done even better. I believe the Lotus team would have survived and Collins would still be running it.'

As it happened, however, Hakkinen 'had a lot of offers, an amazing amount of offers', but went to McLaren. It was a calculated risk, with the accent heavily on risk – in any language you want.

• CHAPTER FIVE •

Deliverance at Brewery Bend

MCLAREN HAD BEEN running with Honda engines since 1988, and in that time had won the World Championship four times (Senna 1988, Prost 1989, Senna 1990 and 1991). There are many other statistics that proclaim the success of what the partnership achieved, and I'll only cite a couple: 53 pole positions and 44 race victories. Having lost Honda, McLaren now faced a season with Formula 1's trusty standby, the Ford. Renault was the dominant engine and it seemed highly unlikely that, across a full season, even McLaren's expertise and Senna's genius could compensate for the Ford's lack of comparable power. Senna contemplated taking the season off. Would he? Wouldn't he? That was the risk Hakkinen took. McLaren had already signed Michael Andretti from IndyCar racing, itself a risk for both McLaren and Andretti himself, given the intrinsic differences in the two forms of racing. What it meant, however, was that if Senna did race, Hakkinen would be reduced to no more than a test driver.

So why McLaren, why the risk?

'A lot of the influence was from Keke, who had driven for McLaren [and finished his Formula 1 career with the team, in 1986]. What was important was that Keke judged Ron Dennis as one of the best team managers in Formula 1, so that was an influence – and Ron's offer wasn't bad either. [Much chuckling] We still didn't know what Senna was going to do. That was not crucial – if he didn't race I'd have had a whole season, but I wasn't counting on that. I was counting on other things: I'm young, I have speed, what's the rush? If I have to be only a test driver for one year . . .'

I have never before heard a Formula 1 driver say 'What's the rush'. Formula 1 is the rush.

136

'Keke was really worried, and you could see how it might have gone. *One year testing! If you stay a test driver for one year, people will crucify you! That's it, your career is finished, you're a test driver, you're not a race driver any more – yes, finished!* But we didn't think this way. I thought *McLaren are a big, successful team, they won't replace me, they cannot put me outside, they are going to have to give me races.*

'I even flew to Kyalami for the first race of the season, the South African Grand Prix, with the feeling that I was going to race – which could have happened. I was sitting there three, four days before the meeting and I was feeling *I'm going to race, I'm going to race.* I had information from *there* and *there* and *there* that Senna wouldn't come. I got myself ready and I was preparing to go for it. Then just before the Grand Prix, *bang*, Ayrton comes back. It hit me really hard. I was looking forward to the race so much and now I couldn't be in it. What to do? Lift yourself up again, tell yourself *so now I'm a tester, I'll go for that.* However, most of the time at Kyalami I had thick sunglasses – I wore them all the weekend – because I was so disappointed and people couldn't see my eyes and see how disappointed I was. I felt so sad.'

Did you watch the race?

'Of course.'

What about when they were on the grid waiting for the green light?

'I was looking at Michael Andretti. He wasn't in a good position [fifth row] and I was thinking *I could do better. Of course I could do better. I know what to do. Why didn't they give me a chance? I'm a good driver –* but, because life is not as simple as that, I had to accept it.'

Andretti was a mistake.

'Andretti needed more time.'

Curiously, what Andretti needed was what you were doing. You should have raced and he should have done the testing, then come into the races when he was acclimatised and ready.

'Correct, correct. The pressure was too much on him, the pressure was too much. I could see that.'

Did you think he would last the whole season?

'Well, the time he had the accident in Brazil [second race of the season, Andretti colliding with Berger at the start] I thought *this cannot last very long, it just cannot.* Every Grand Prix that came along, I wasn't hoping he'd be out or Ayrton [now settled to driving in all of them] would be out, I was just hoping I'd be in.'

A few days before the Portuguese Grand Prix, 14th round of this 1993 World Championship, Andretti departed McLaren and returned to his native United States. He hadn't finished seven times and won only seven points. After the months of testing and patient waiting, Hakkinen came in to partner Senna. I know that, for all sorts of reasons, a Formula 1 driver would never admit to being daunted by a direct comparison with Senna, but in Hakkinen's case I am sure he wasn't. He said, 'I'm not in awe of him but I love being his team-mate,' which was fair enough. What proves my contention is this:

Friday free practice	Hakkinen	1m 13.857	(2nd overall)
	Senna	1m 13.868	(3rd)

Qualifying	Senna	1m 12.954	(3rd)
	Hakkinen	1m 12.956	(4th)
Saturday free practice	Senna	1m 13.434	(2nd)
	Hakkinen	1m 13.817	(4th)
Qualifying	Hakkinen	1m 12.443	(2nd)
	Senna	1m 12.491	(3rd)

It put Hakkinen on the second row of the grid (Hill, pole, and Prost on the front) but ahead of Senna, something regarded as a genuine

Sometimes it's important to get away from it all and relax (Keke Rosberg/Wake-Upp Productions).

sensation and momentarily eclipsing the news that Prost, who could win the World Championship at this race, had announced his retirement and Senna seemed certain to replace him at Williams the following season.

'I was confident like hell,' Hakkinen says. 'Really confident. I went there and I wanted to win. I knew the car, I knew the team, so it was my chance to prove what I could do. I did prove it. I went quicker than Ayrton, which was a good thing.'

He didn't like things like that.

'He didn't like things like that. After qualifying, in one way it was bad, it was a terrible feeling because Ayrton was with his engineer, Giorgio Ascanelli, he was sitting on top of the tyres in the garage next to the computers. Ayrton could not understand how this was possible. How could this happen? He couldn't accept it. He was studying the computer; he couldn't understand a couple of corners where this Hakkinen had been quicker.'

Did you speak to him afterwards?

'I did. I did, yes.'

Did he say anything that we could put in the book?

'No. We had jokes about it, but that was later . . .'

(An insight from John Alcorn that may not be inappropriate at this point: joining McLaren, he insists, had not changed Hakkinen. 'When I'd finished racing and Mika was at Lotus, a nicer guy you could never wish to meet, and I've seen him a few times at McLaren. Since I was racing against Damon and the others, the only two that always came rushing over if they saw me were Mark Blundell and Mika. That proves what nice guys they were because I'm nothing any more; I couldn't be of any benefit to them or anything else.')

Now Hakkinen had caused the sensation. 'We had a good fight in qualifying and I was sweating a little afterwards, but Finnish sweat is very dry,' he said. (Relax. I don't know what it means, either.)

The race, over 191 miles (308km), would inevitably make other demands, although Hill had trouble getting away from the dummy grid and started from the back. That gave Hakkinen an unobstructed path forward from the second row. At the green light he quickly drew abreast of Prost and edged him towards the grass verge, a move that Prost did not appreciate. Meanwhile Jean Alesi in the Ferrari surged round the outside to lead, Hakkinen second, Senna third and staying very, very close to Hakkinen. He was about to give Hakkinen a lesson in racing: he feinted right and Hakkinen blocked that by going right himself, then he darted through on the left and from there, pursuing Alesi, drew away from Hakkinen.

Senna's engine let go after 19 laps, and Hakkinen's pit stop dropped him to fifth, but he was up to fourth after 32 laps when, rounding the fast horseshoe corner on to the start-finish straight, he went wide, skipped across the narrow strip of grass and thundered the barrier, the car bucking. It was pitched back across the track and thundered the barrier at the other side. Hakkinen emerged unhurt and said he'd probably been too close to Alesi and lost downforce.

'I had to push like hell in the corners because I didn't have the power on the straight. The Ford is not a bad engine but it is lacking in power and I couldn't stay with the Ferrari. I was in sixth gear, just coming up to the rev limiter, when the car went wide. When it was on top of the kerb I knew it wasn't coming back if I turned the wheel, so I decided to steer it on to the grass, then try to come back on to the track. I kept my foot down. Unfortunately there was a massive dip in the grass and that threw the front end into the air and the left rear into the wall. I went across the track and the right front hit the other side. The only thing that worried me was when I was going sideways down the track, I could

The astonishing debut for McLaren at Estoril, which ended like this (Pascal Rondeau/Allsport).

see the front wheel [which had been wrenched off] bouncing straight towards me with the wishbones sticking out. That was scary. Luckily, it stopped 10 metres before it reached me.'

A postscript or two. Jo Ramirez wondered if Hakkinen had had a problem early on when he couldn't stay with Senna, and typically Hakkinen was extremely honest. The problem wasn't doing one hot lap, as he had done in qualifying, but sustaining a heightened pace, which is not the same thing. (Julian Bailey says, 'I think Senna had been de-motivated somewhat up to that point in the season, and in qualifying Hakkinen pulled him up a bit. In the race Senna absolutely annihilated Hakkinen, annihilated him. That would have been the true test for me, whether Hakkinen could have *raced* Senna, and he couldn't.')

Some time shortly after, I had to ring Rosberg in Monaco about another matter altogether, and before I could broach even that he's recounting how he had expensive tickets for an open-air boxing match in Cardiff, flew to London with his wife, remembered that Britain in autumn invariably means rain, thought to hell with freezing and soaking in Cardiff, hired a Rolls-Royce and toured London instead, bought fish and chips and had forgotten how terrible they taste. In conversation with Rosberg, this is the way it goes.

Anyway, when he finally paused to draw breath I wondered if something had broken on Hakkinen's McLaren or whether it was driver error. Keke Rosberg is – like Hakkinen himself – one of those very rare people who invariably speak their minds. *Driver error*, Rosberg said, short and sharp.

In the background I could hear another voice muttering.

Driver error, Rosberg repeated, louder.

Not driver error, the background voice, now audibly that of Hakkinen, said.

Driver error!

Not driver error!

Yes, this is the way it goes with Rosberg.

Reflecting now, Hakkinen is completely, touchingly honest. 'When we came to the race itself I realised what a long way I still had to go to reach the level where Ayrton was.

'What Jo says is fair. It comes with experience and Ayrton was already three times World Champion and I hadn't even won a Grand Prix ever, never even been on the podium ever. Ayrton did open my eyes that day. I said to myself *Jesus, I have a long way to go.*

'The problem is that if you are young in a business like this, if you don't work yourself really hard, if you're not ready both physically and psychologically, it can do bad things for you – a lot of damage. I tell you, you have to be *really, really* ready. If you are fighting against a man like Ayrton Senna, it is no joke. It is such serious stuff. People at that level are so bloody good and that means only one thing. You have to make yourself better.'

I knew I could overtake a couple of cars at the start – that absolutely was my thinking

At season's end Prost retired, Senna transferred to Williams and Martin Brundle joined McLaren from Ligier. The season of 1994 is etched in dark shadow: Senna and Roland Ratzenberger killed at Imola, safety suddenly an obsession and, on a more prosaic level, McLaren and their Peugeot engine off the pace. By mid-season Hakkinen had only seven points and Brundle six (compared to Schumacher, leading the Championship, with 72). Moreover, on the last lap of the British Grand Prix, Hakkinen and Rubens Barrichello (Jordan) tangled; Hakkinen left the circuit in the other sense of that term – changed and departed – without the permission of the stewards and was given a suspended one-race ban.

The start of the next race, Germany at Hockenheim, was dominated by an extensive, acrimonious and controversial crash. Hakkinen qualified on the fourth row, next to Mark Blundell (Tyrrell) but 'behind' him because of the stagger of the grid. Although Blundell had been driving against Hakkinen since 1991 he scarcely knew him except as just another driver. What, I asked Blundell, are you thinking as the cars come slowly round on the parade lap to form the grid?

'Apart from checking the basics of making sure the car is operational – in terms of gears and clutch and brakes, but that's just reassurance – you are sizing up what you are going to do into the first corner. You are very aware of who is around you on the grid. You're pumped up, you have so much adrenalin flowing through you that you try and keep yourself relaxed but you can't. You've got butterflies . . .'

Sign language, with engineer Giorgio Ascanelli in 1994 (Photos by Matthias Schneider, courtesy BOSS).

What was Hakkinen thinking?

'I knew I could overtake a couple of cars at the start. That absolutely was my thinking. I never think I can lose two places at the start. I don't know which two cars they are going to be that I overtake – although they are always cars in front of me. [Chuckle broadens to laughter] Automatically you anticipate that they will be the cars on the row in front of you.'

It was a warm afternoon at Hockenheim and the 26 cars settled into the bays on the grid, the twin columns stretching back to an official with a green flag who scampered across the back of the grid waving it: all present and correct. Blundell was in the left-hand column, Hakkinen in the right and nearest the pit lane wall. The 26 faced the short, sharp surge to the first corner, a right-hander. The pit lane wall would be running alongside them on their right with a white boundary line in front of it – this is the side of the track that, for purposes of overtaking, the drivers call *inside*. Conversely – when the green lights released the 26 cars, and the twin columns broke up in the rush to the first corner – any of those cars veering left were taking the *outside*.

The bank of three red lights came on.

Blundell's view: 'They don't suddenly go green. What happens is that the reds go off and you accelerate then. It's quicker. You *don't* wait for the green . . .'

All this happened so fast that even replaying the start frame by frame on a video does not reveal the difference. It's all a sort of molten moment, moving from the static to the frantic virtually instantaneously. These days, of course, there isn't a green any more, just reds that go off.

'I have a technique in the start that is very quick, quicker than others,' Hakkinen says. 'It's good for that, good for being quicker.' Anyway, 'green light, *booom*.'

Blundell's view: 'You go over the line and you're immediately looking for where a gap might be. Where is that gap? Where am I going to make up places?'

Hakkinen, of course, fully intended to make up two places. 'It's normal to overtake inside. You don't want to go outside because if something happens that's where the pieces fly. If cars spin, they'll be spinning there so you want to go inside, and inside also means that when you reach the first corner you are on a good line to go round it.

That's the most important thing. So I wanted to be on the inside line.' The McLaren jerked left but he flicked it right. 'I go inside deliberately. Second gear, *booom.*'

Blundell's view: 'As soon as you have got away from the line you assess how you've got away. Are you carrying too much wheelspin? Has the thing gone sideways on you? And is there somebody who's already drawn up to the side of you? Your field of vision is 180 degrees covering what's in front of you and what's around you.'

Both Hakkinen and Blundell saw gaps. Hakkinen crossed the white boundary line in front of the pit lane wall and ran towards the first corner; Blundell twisted the Tyrrell to mid-track. They had David Coulthard (Williams) between them. At this instant, much further back, Andrea de Cesaris (Sauber), Alessandro Zanardi (Lotus) and both the Minardis – driven by Alboreto and Pierluigi Martini – crashed, spearing left and right off the track like a bomb-burst. Everyone else fled on towards the first corner.

The car was full of fuel, heavy like a tank – you can see the wall coming

---

Blundell's view: 'You're not really aware of what's going on behind you.'

Hakkinen had a clear channel, but Blundell, finding himself alongside Coulthard and closing, flicked away, flicked back again, and Coulthard was sandwiched by Hakkinen so close outside him. Coulthard and Blundell rubbed wheels, flicked apart.

'I don't know who was in front of me,' Hakkinen says, 'but he began to push me on to the white close to the pit wall. I went over the line and I was going closer and closer to the wall. I had no alternative. OK, I could have backed off completely, but that would have created more danger because somebody could have hit me in the back. So I went for it, I just went for it. I did overtake two cars, I was heading for the first corner . . .'

Blundell's view: 'Hakkinen was technically out of the circuit when he went over the white line by the pit lane wall. I saw him and Coulthard closing in. I thought *they're getting closer and closer and closer, this is going to be a major drama.* I saw them touch. It happens at fantastic speed, but to a driver it seems at a slower rate. Mentally the driver slows everything down. You're hard on the throttle, you're aware of everything, it's all real-time speed but somehow unconsciously you have slowed it down.'

Hakkinen turned across the front of Coulthard. 'Automatically when you come to the first corner you start taking a racing line – coming back across, in fact,' Hakkinen says. 'What happens then? Coulthard touches my rear wheel. You can feel the touch, but it is weak, very weak. I lose control.' The touch pitched the McLaren in a great slewing motion across the track, reaching towards Blundell in a diagonal.

Blundell's view: 'Next thing, I am hard on my brakes because there is a guy about to sideswipe me in the biggest possible way. You think *made it! He's missed me!* Suddenly from behind, *whaaam*, somebody's rammed me – nothing I could have done about that at all.' It was Barrichello (Jordan) who could do nothing at all, either.

Hakkinen, still at the diagonal, shrieked across the track. 'I go sideways like *this* and I've 20 cars coming at me like *this* and I'm looking at them like *this.*'

Is it possible to think, 'I'll be OK, they won't hit me'?

'You just hope they won't hit you. That's what you think, not *I'm OK.*' Anyway, 'I go off, that's it.' Hakkinen now shrieked over the gravel run-off area at immense speed, leaving a trail of wreckage, smoke and dust. 'The only problem at that time was that I knew the car was full of fuel, it was heavy like a tank. It won't stop and it didn't stop. You can see the wall coming. Then you hit the wall. Then you are sliding flat out against the wall, *baaang.*'

The car bounced from a tyre wall, its left side savaged, its left-hand wheels wrenched off.

Blundell's view: 'Mika was wrong, but I also felt that Coulthard wasn't using his head. His Williams was far superior to all the other cars on the race-track, and he only needed to lift off the accelerator for a fraction of a second to avoid trouble. If Hakkinen had taken the corner before he – Coulthard – did, at a track like Hockenheim it wouldn't have taken him more than four or five laps to overtake. You had two young guys and there was a lack of experience. What made Hakkinen do it? I guess it was that channelled instinct that he must get to the first corner before everybody else, which is all well and good, but . . .'

The track resembled a battleground.

Hakkinen was given a one-race ban. In self-defence he said at the

The start of the Hockenheim crashes. There's chaos at the back of the grid as the cars move towards the first corner. Hakkinen is just out of sight on the left (ICN U.K. Bureau).

time, 'When I started to brake and change down for the corner I felt a hit on the rear tyre and lost control. You try to block it out, but you can't help thinking about it.' Reflecting now, he says, 'Let me put it this way: to have a crash like that you need two people, never one. You always need two people. Hockenheim we had six people off the track – quite a few on the first corner, and I was one of them. Because I went off first, of course, I got the first blame. Nevertheless, whatever happened there was a reason for it.'

(I asked Hughie Absalom, who understands the mentality and motives of drivers, to reflect on how Hockenheim could happen. Is there a bit of a devil inside Hakkinen? 'Yes, but I think a lot of these people are like that. I can give you a specific example. It was a Formula 3 race at Thruxton when Mika was driving for Dick Bennetts; he was on the front row and he stalled or something. He was last away, but by the end he had passed everybody except the winner. That's not normal. If you look at the whole of Formula 3 I believe only two drivers have ever done that, Hakkinen and Barrichello.' Of that day at Thruxton, *Autosport* said, 'Astounding is the only word to describe Hakkinen's performance.')

Hakkinen finished this 1994 season fourth in the Championship with 26 points. He felt the season could be divided, 'from the start until

Hockenheim when I drove flat out all the time and inevitably made a few mistakes, and the second half where I kept in mind the lessons I had learned in the first part of the year.'

For 1995 McLaren had Mercedes engines and ought to have had Nigel Mansell (returned from IndyCars) partnering Hakkinen, but Nigel couldn't fit in the car so the team reached for the test driver, Blundell. 'I didn't know him [Mika] until we met in 1995,' Blundell says, 'and the circumstances under which we met were difficult, anyway, with the Mansell situation and the way that I came in. I knew the guillotine was hanging over me. I didn't have any illusions about that. I was driving on a race-by-race contract and Mika was well-established at McLaren.

'My first impression? Mika is a nice guy, no two ways about that, but he always seemed to be shielded. He had people around him who were very protective of him, which was interesting to see because I'd never had anything like that. I'm very much *there's me and there's me and that's it*. I come from a different sort of background and I carry myself quite differently to the way he does. He had an enormous pressure on him, in fact an enormous amount of responsibility at a very young age. McLaren were a major team and Mika was deemed to be the lead driver. Even when Nigel Mansell was there I still feel the emphasis was on Mika to be lead guy. One thing you *have* to say about him, he's very quick. Very, very quick. He has an unorthodox driving style that depends on left-foot braking . . .'

In a ordinary right-hand-drive road-going car you have three pedals – clutch on the left, brake and accelerator on the right – the idea being that you take your right foot *off* the accelerator to brake. Same idea on a Formula 1 car with this difference: the clutch is not a pedal, it's a button on the steering wheel, leaving the brake and accelerator pedals for the right foot. A racing driver's left foot gets the afternoon off, except Hakkinen's.

'The braking pedal,' Blundell says, 'is positioned out at the left-hand side of the monocoque and he doesn't have a heel bar. He is constantly hovering his foot over this left pedal to brake, almost the rally style, almost rock 'n' roll: he keeps his right foot on the accelerator *while* he applies brake load. He'd apply it in the style of a go-kart, punch the car hard to get the rear end moving out. He'd go into a corner like that.

'I must admit that at McLaren I tried to emulate how he drove it

Left *The aftermath* (Mike Hewitt/Allsport).

because for obvious reasons it made it easier for the team to have cars that were the same. I couldn't get used to it. In the circumstances in which I arrived in the team – I was only told I was going to the first Grand Prix eight days before [because Mansell couldn't fit] – I didn't really have time to get used to it and you go back to what you feel confident with.'

This matter is intriguing and I asked Hakkinen about it. 'Left-foot braking is a technique that comes from karting times. That's where you learn to do it. Now, in a Formula 1 car you change gear with a button on the steering wheel, and that's what is difficult because you are relying a lot on computers. It's not *feeling*, just click on the button and it does it; but sometimes the computer doesn't want to do it.

'I don't want to talk about it too much, and why I don't want to talk about it too much is because at the moment I don't do left-foot braking, I do right-foot braking. Left-foot is very difficult, very tricky and maybe I go back to it some day.'

What is it? You accelerate with the right foot while you brake with the left, balancing the two?

'There is no balance. You go throttle-then-brake, throttle-then-brake. A very, very tricky business – fantastic if you can do it, fantastic if you understand how to do it. But it takes time to learn it, and the problem in Formula 1 is that you don't have much time to learn it: you don't want to sacrifice three or four grands prix trying to find out. The truth is, *the more you use left-foot braking the more you come to know how difficult it is.* If it is working, it gives your body a good balance in the car and it's a nice way of driving. Imagine writing left-handed if you are naturally right-handed. You could do it if you had been practising from five years old – not as well as with the right hand, but you could at least do it. Afterwards, if you start the practising when you're a bit older, it's too late. If I hadn't done it in karts I would never be able to learn it now.'

This is how the 1995 season unfolded: in Brazil Hakkinen qualified on the fourth row, Blundell the fifth; Hakkinen finished fourth, Blundell sixth. In Argentina Hakkinen qualified on the third row, Blundell the ninth; Hakkinen collided with Eddie Irvine immediately in the race, Blundell out after nine laps, engine. Mansell displaced Blundell for Imola and Spain, then departed, leaving Blundell to do a solid job for the rest of the season.

'In terms of outright speed,' Blundell says, 'Mika was quick, but his level of consistency that year was debatable at times. He could run very, very quickly for a period, but then he'd drop off for a bit. I think Mika was also very much driven by what was going on around him. If someone important, someone of big stature, walked through the garage during qualifying it would result in Mika doing a lap time half a second quicker. There had been no changes on the car. He had extracted that half a second from himself just to put some personal emphasis in there, which is good but it can also be very bad in testing where you may need to be extracting that half a second all the time. That was a little bit of a worry factor but, you know, that was him. You had to understand him, and that was how he was.

'I knew I wasn't going to be the Number 1 guy and I also knew I wasn't getting the Number 1 equipment. Ninety-nine per cent of the time he was probably a spec in front of me on the engines.' This is traditional motor sport ground and naturally, if Mercedes (in this case) produced a new specification engine, the Number 1 driver ought to have first use of it. Blundell had been in it long enough to know all about the logic of that.

'You just have to go out there and do your best. To the outside world I may have seemed off the pace, but you look at what really happened. I ran Mika close on a number of occasions in qualifying and it would take him all his time – you know, the last lap of qualifying – to pull that extra bit out bearing in mind, as I have said, he was probably a spec in front on engines. I could really *feel* he was pushing, pushing all the time to the point where I out-qualified him at Estoril, where he had out-qualified Senna only two years before. He felt it, he felt it big time.'

Portugal was round 13 and by then – in fact the race before, Monza – Hakkinen had finished a strong second to Herbert, the first time he'd been on the podium in the season. At Portugal Blundell qualified on the sixth row (1m 22.914s), Hakkinen next but on the seventh row (1m 23.064s).

Did that affect your relationship?

'For me, no, because it's not in my nature. I've done a good job, I'm happy, I'm happy for my guys, I'm happy for my engineer, and that's it, let's get on with it, tomorrow's race day,' Blundell says. 'Mika was a young guy and there was still some of the child in him – if you want to put it like that – which now and again would burst out. In certain ways

I could understand it, but in other ways I didn't actually agree with it. If I was to burst out with some emotions it wouldn't look right, wouldn't even feel right. There would be certain things going on just to let me know that he was boss. Silly little things. Bits and pieces like going for promotional appearances: he'd be late and I'd have to wait or, if the two of us had to do it, *well, I'm going in first, I want to do that, I want to get it out of the way* and so on and so on. Fine. I'm over 21. It doesn't worry me, you know.'

He could not know that within seconds his life would be in grave danger

---

A question to Hakkinen. *Do you, in a quiet but firm way, make sure everybody knows your status?*

'No. As for making people wait, I have my programme, my schedule, and I always try and do everything as smoothly as possible: not as fast as possible, as smoothly as possible in a professional way.'

I'm thinking about a team-mate who might be a threat to you. How do you react to that?

'Results, results, results. I let the results speak for themselves usually.'

Have you ever tried psychologically?

'Yeah. I've tried everything.'

Who did you try it with?

'All the drivers . . .'

Blundell says that 'Estoril was a good turning point. He already had some respect for me because he knew if I was anywhere near him [in qualifying] I was doing a pretty good job, to the point at Estoril where he actually contemplated overnight changing his pedals for the race to go back to what I was using. He couldn't quite believe I had out-qualified him.'

Hakkinen didn't finish the race (an engine problem) and Blundell slogged to ninth; and qualifying was tight for the European Grand Prix at the Nurburgring (Hakkinen 1m 20.866s, Blundell 1m 20.909s). Hakkinen didn't compete in the Pacific at Aida, Japan – he was recovering from an appendix operation – but finished second again in Japan and flew down to Adelaide.

On Friday 10 November 1995 he eased the McLaren out of the pits and began to put together a qualifying run round the 3.7 kilometres of the circuit. At strategic points six medical cars waited poised to go to any emergency. Each had a driver with a motor racing licence (so if they had to go fast they'd know what they were doing), an ambulanceman with additional paramedic skills, and two doctors. Since the doctors were all unpaid volunteers, their specialist skills inevitably varied.

Hakkinen rounded the 90-degree right-hander that led on to Rundle Road – down to third gear, down to 100kph, carrying 1.8 G-loading – and accelerated.

He could not know that, within seconds, his life would be in grave and increasing danger, nor that two of the best men to save it were standing beside the medical car – the white estate – that was positioned behind the armco on the left. Doctors Jerome Cockings and Stephen Lewis were in their early 30s and both lovers of the sport. They worked at the Royal Adelaide Hospital, which, almost literally, was just around the corner, Cockings an intensive care specialist with extensive knowledge of anaesthetics, Lewis a trained neurosurgeon (that's operating on the nervous system, but especially the brain and spine).

Lewis was 'taking time off work because I had an interest in the sport. I do a lot of local races round the place just to have some medical presence there.'

Cockings, a Briton, had 'always had an interest in motor sport and I'd been a medical officer in a similar sort of fashion at Brands Hatch for some years, predominantly at motor bike meetings, before I left the UK.'

They had worked together for some years in intensive care at the Royal Adelaide, were preoccupied with head injuries and, Lewis says, 'as a result we requested that, if it was at all possible, we would like to be posted in the same car at the circuit. That happened and it was good because we were familiar with working together. Friends? Yes, definitely.'

Hakkinen came round the corner, the sleek nose of the McLaren pointed down the gully of Rundle Road, the car digging speed from the mighty Mercedes engine. Almost absently, Lewis thought *Crickey, if anything does happen we are ideally suited here. Between us, we could operate on somebody right on the track.* Cockings watched Hakkinen come, the speed of the McLaren rising so urgently from the right-hander, but it was just another car of the 24 taking part in this first

Serenity at Spa (Mike Cooper/Allsport).

qualifying, just another approach, nothing more. As the jaw of Brewery Bend opened to it, the McLaren slewed, the left rear tyre punctured. Cockings saw Hakkinen 'lose control'.

Lewis heard 'this great squeal of tyres, looked up and saw the thing spinning round and hitting the barrier. You know instantly that someone is not well because they just don't move. As soon as they move their heads you think *Ah, there's something there.*'

At the moment of impact Hakkinen's head had been hammered down against the steering wheel with frantic, terrible ferocity, had rebounded from that, then thrashed left-right, then lolled virtually motionless. The car had come to rest broadside on to the blue and yellow tyre barrier that had a waist-high concrete wall behind it. Of the three marshals situated behind this, one had already scaled the tyre barrier and was lowering himself towards the car, and a second was over the concrete wall. As he turned, stooped and lifted a red fire extinguisher from behind the wall, the first marshal was on his knees craning into the cockpit. From further away four fire-fighters cantered in a line hard towards the McLaren.

'The marshals,' Lewis says, 'did absolutely everything right: held the guy's head steady. That's a first principle, because you worry about a neck fracture and so on.'

Hakkinen would have 'no memory of actually hitting the wall', but did remember 'sitting in the car immediately afterwards and not being able to see anything.' He does remember, too, 'sitting in the cockpit and I could not move my arms. I made a conscious effort to move them again, and again I could not. That was when I knew it must have been a big shunt. I said to myself *relax, do not panic. There is nothing you can*

do and the medical people will know what they are doing. How could I react like this? Well, there is no point in panicking. That's the way I am. I am able to react like that. Normally it is little things that irritate me and I react strongly to them. I don't think it is because I'm Finnish and the Finns are unemotional. It's just the way I am.'

The on-board radio from race control came to life, instructing the medical car to go to the crash. This is an important consideration. Medical cars – in this case the white estate – do not go out among

The crash with Rubens Barrichello at the end of the British Grand Prix, 1995 (ICN U.K. Bureau).

The deliverance at Brewery Bend (all Pascal Rondeau/ Allsport).

Left *The car snaps out of control.*

The car has come to rest amidst the tyres.

Lifting him out.

The lifesavers.

racing cars without specific orders to do so, even though here the medical car would be moving from one side of the Brewery Bend triangle – where three roads met, remember – to another side without having to go round the track.

Cockings says that the job of the first marshal to arrive is carrying out tasks like removing the steering wheel, releasing the driver's seat belts and extinguishing any fire. Now, 'immediately the marshal reached the car he realised Hakkinen was unresponsive, had clearly been injured and that it was a big one. By that time we were driving there. It is policy and procedure and it is normal reaction to get in the medical car and drive.'

If the oxygen supply had remained low he would have suffered brain damage, if not death

---

Lewis emphasises the point. 'We always take the car, *always* take the car even though an incident might be as this one was, within walking or quick-running distance. You always take the car because at the scene it is set up at an angle to protect us and protect the racing driver from oncoming racing cars. It becomes a barricade and a strategic part of the whole exercise. It's common sense. You don't work on or near a track where racing cars are still circulating without having the vehicle there so that a) the drivers can see it and b) you are protected.' The estate drew up in the protective position and Cockings and Lewis emerged moving in a controlled scamper, one to each side of the McLaren.

Cockings estimates that this was within 15 seconds of impact. He found Hakkinen 'sitting upright in the McLaren losing a lot of blood from his mouth. His eyes were open but unresponsive, not a conscious open. He had hit his head pretty hard and that rendered him unable to move. The principle is that the oxygen and the blood supply must be preserved, particularly to the brain. It is the most important aspect at that stage. Otherwise you have brain damage very quickly. How long? Probably from around 2, 3 minutes.'

Others opened the boot of the medical car and began bringing equipment out. A second medical vehicle – a van – drew up, butting on to the medical car, increasing the barricade. This van had a specialist extrication crew in it.

Lewis: 'I put the old knuckle press into his chest [clenching your hand into a fist so the knuckles protrude] as some sort of stimulant to see if it got any reaction. Hakkinen was certainly out for the count, not doing a thing. We realised when our initial *Hello, how are you? What's happening?* met with no response that he was seriously injured. We could see the blood coming out of his mouth. We took his helmet off carefully and gave him oxygen . . .'

Cockings: 'We applied a mask with a high flow of oxygen to his face while other people arranged to start lifting him out. The important thing was that we could do very little to him while he was in the car. A priority is to get him out and lay him down so you can get at him properly. It was important to keep his neck straight. That sort of incident can very easily mean a neck injury as well. I held his head and neck still and the others caught him under the arms and under the legs and lifted him *straight*. The ambulance people are particularly good at it. They get used to working together so that everyone lifts in unison and his spine doesn't move as such.'

Hakkinen was laid on the ground next to the McLaren.

Lewis: 'We got into our basic life support stuff. Time means a lot, you've got to get on with it, and what you do first of all is make sure that enough air is going in. It's simple A, B, Cs. He wasn't ventilating himself so we went through the routine that we normally do.'

Cockings: 'The degree of unconsciousness is always hard to confirm, but essentially he was unable to move, unable to breathe and unable to communicate in any way. He was, however, definitely alive. He still had a pulse.'

Yes, but you'd had the 2, 3 minutes, but getting him out of the car and lying him down had eaten into that.

'Indeed, indeed. The priority is to get access for oxygen and machinery to ventilate the lungs. That was not possible in the usual way, through his mouth, because you couldn't open his mouth. It was locked closed; that was part of the trauma and injury to his head, and it's not uncommon. Then he started to turn blue, a sort of greyish blue, which really indicated that the oxygen supply was running very low. We were approaching that time when, if the oxygen supply had remained low, he would certainly have suffered brain damage, if not death. I made a small incision over the trachea with a surgical knife from a kit we always have in the car specifically designed for that

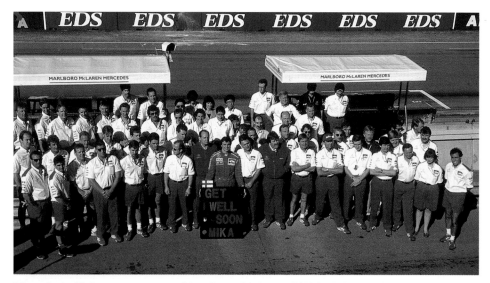

The whole McLaren team, speaking from the heart (ICN U.K. Bureau).

purpose. I then passed a tube in and we delivered the oxygen via that. Immediately his colour improved and his condition stabilised. He couldn't be given anaesthetic because for that you need something into a vein and it was too early, nobody had had a chance.'

Mistily, Hakkinen remembers 'feeling pain, and I couldn't move, but I understood what was going on and I remember telling myself to relax, just to let the medical people do their job. Certainly I understood I was hurt quite badly, and it was getting difficult to breathe. Then I felt this massive pain in my throat, which I guess was when they put the tube in, and at that point I lost consciousness.' Oddly, perhaps, he also remembers 'a sort of choking, which I think was when the tube was put into my throat' – when the opposite was happening.

Lewis: 'I cut through Hakkinen's driving suit with heavy-duty scissors I carry in my pocket especially for that and put a line in. We put drips into this arm and gave him fluids so he had good air going in to his lungs and fluid going into his body to combat any problems that shock might have produced, but of course we didn't know if there were any other injuries, to his tummy or anything.'

The drugs ended the muscle spasm.

Cockings: 'That enabled us to get a better tube in through his mouth because the drugs relaxed the mouth. We could open it to get the tube in. He was orally intubated. By then a number of people had arrived to help us, including The Prof [Professor Sid Watkins, Formula 1's resident travelling doctor]. It was interesting. By the time we had stabilised everything we had been there for several minutes, and it was only really then that I looked up to see who else was around helping me. I found the person I had been asking things of and who had been passing things to me was The Prof! It would have been very easy, I think, for him to have tried to assume control, but he was prepared to let us get on doing what we were doing. I have admiration for him.'

After some 15 minutes Hakkinen was lifted into an ambulance. Cockings and Lewis got in too, and it drove down Rundle Road, but turned off at the 90-degree right-hander. The Royal Adelaide Hospital was a couple of hundred yards further on, and the whole journey took only around a minute. On arrival Hakkinen was rapidly assessed for any other life-threatening injuries, his head scanned, and he was transferred to intensive care where, as it happened, Lewis's 'particular unit of neurosurgery was on duty, so Mika ended up being my patient! It was almost like *how much more of this?!*'

That evening Cockings wasn't on call, but he stayed around, talking at length with Lewis about what they had done and how things were progressing. Cockings points out that 'it's actually not that often when doctors find themselves in a position where their actions are quite clearly the difference between life and death' in such a stark, immediate way as they had been with Hakkinen.

Sedated, Hakkinen remained unconscious until the following morning when, as we heard at the start of this book, he came round and made the walking motion across his chest with his fingers.

Cockings: 'We were very pleased when, the following day, he was clearly making such a good recovery, but that was still an early stage to say he was going to make a complete and full recovery. There is obviously a very big difference between being alive and being back in racing form. It would only have taken a subtle type of brain injury to have taken his racing edge off, perhaps.'

Lewis: 'It's a very difficult thing to get a grip of what's going on in the brain, particularly after an incident. You can't see it, you can't feel it, it's hidden by the skull. The best indicator is talking to a patient. *How are you going? Can you lift up your arms and legs?* But these patients are unconscious. How do you know what's going on? One of the quests around the world in my field has been to find better ways of following all these critical things inside the head and being able to monitor them. And he had suffered a hell of an impact, 180–200 kilometres an hour. He shifted the concrete wall behind the tyre barrier back a foot. He pushed the whole thing back. The little control buttons on the steering wheel dented his crash helmet, so it really had gone forward. The steering wheel was broken. The crash helmet actually fractured the steering wheel. That's how hard the impact was.'

Hakkinen remembers coming round again – not the walking of the fingers, but later – and 'looking up at Professor Watkins'. It was 'a very strong moment. He asked if I could understand him, and I said *yes*. Then he asked me to touch my fingers and so on, which I did. Ron Dennis was there with his wife Lisa, who was holding my hand all the time. It was the first moment I began to feel strong. Sid looked at me very carefully and said, "Mika, you have been very fortunate because you are not going to need any brain surgery." I was relieved of course, but also a little bit shocked, realising how badly I had been injured, how lucky I was to be alive. Once I'd heard these words the important thing was to show everyone that I was basically OK. I could see on people's faces that they couldn't hide their emotion, their worry, and I tried to be positive in any way I could. In fact, when my girlfriend Erja arrived at the hospital I insisted on telling her a naughty joke I'd heard the day before the accident.'

This coming round is precisely fixed in Hakkinen's memory, and so are the rounded, civilised modulations of Professor Watkins's voice explaining how lucky he had been. There was something Hakkinen needed urgently to know: *did I make a mistake, was it my mistake?* The evidence is clear, particularly when accompanied by the film from the on-board camera. Debris caused a tyre to puncture and Hakkinen became essentially a passenger, as helpless as anyone watching the crash from the stands.

As time went by, Lewis noted that visitors to Hakkinen from Formula 1 were absolutely fascinated by the equipment monitoring the brain. 'We record data every 5 seconds or so. Their comment was *Oh my goodness, look at all the stuff they've got around him – it looks just like one of our engines and its telemetry!* They were very, very intrigued by all the methods we use.

'What made the difference in recovery between him and the normal Joe Blow who has a car accident and gets similar injuries is that we were there so quickly and able to conduct something that was almost like a controlled experiment.'

By early December Hakkinen was spending time in the Botanic Garden beside the Royal Adelaide Hospital. He told Bob Jennings of *The Advertiser*: 'I am very lucky to be in the situation I'm in at the moment. At least I can walk and do things normally, and the doctors say I will make a full recovery. The crash hasn't changed my mind about racing, but at the moment I'm scared – scared of what might happen if I slip and bang my head again. It is still sore and if I do too much "sport" (he was shirtless and had been doing sit-up exercises in the Garden) my head aches. The next one to two months is critical and the doctors tell me I shouldn't hit my head again.' He was also deep into the process of 'thinking a lot about the accident because I want to sort out in my mind exactly what happened'.

There was no hurry to fly him home.

Lewis: 'It was pointless to take any risks and you're talking about

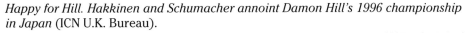

Happy for Hill. Hakkinen and Schumacher annoint Damon Hill's 1996 championship in Japan (ICN U.K. Bureau).

taking him to the northern hemisphere, where it was winter. He was getting all the medical care he needed here. That's why he stayed with us as long as he did, so that he got well. He lost a lot of weight, but that's the whole thing. You can never predict how people will react to injury, particularly head injury. Everybody reacts differently. You may be a fit, well young guy, but you may be devastated by all this and take a long time to recover.'

Hakkinen flew back to London with two doctors in attendance, Lewis one of them. 'Jerome Cockings was meant to be the other one but he'd got a job change and been shifted up to Brisbane. Maybe it was a little bit over the top to have doctors in attendance, but Mika was my patient, I got to know him quite well and he wouldn't leave the country without us! As he said, *this is my career and I don't want anything to go wrong now that I've done so well. You come back with me.'*

They travelled on a scheduled flight ('wasn't any need for any other,' Lewis says) and Hakkinen was delivered into the London Independent Hospital where, under the supervision of Watkins, he had microsurgery to repair 'tiny bones in my ear', then he travelled on to Monaco and home, still accompanied by Lewis – who hadn't been to Europe before and naturally wanted to see as much as he could.

Lewis: 'On the way back I was able to call in for a night and say hello to Keke, have a little chat about it all. This was very pleasant. It was also interesting because Rosberg said *we were sitting here in Monaco watching on television and Mika had the accident. We thought, of all the places in the world, why there, why Australia? You people have shown not only me that I'm ignorant but a lot of other people that they're ignorant, too. You are the same – or better – than us, not only medically but scientifically.'*

A week after arriving back in Monaco, Hakkinen said: 'I still have some problems, of course, but nothing serious. At present I can't swallow as easily as before, but my life is coming back into focus again. Over the last few days I've started to feel normal once more. I feel I would like to go running again, but instead I have to say no, *watch TV, drink apple juice, take it easy.*

'I've been out a lot, walking for miles. When you lie in a hospital bed not eating anything for two weeks basically you just fade away. I lost 10kg and I don't know yet how hard I will have to train to get back to

Right *Always keep your eye on the future* (Photo Wilhelm, courtesy Mercedes-Benz).

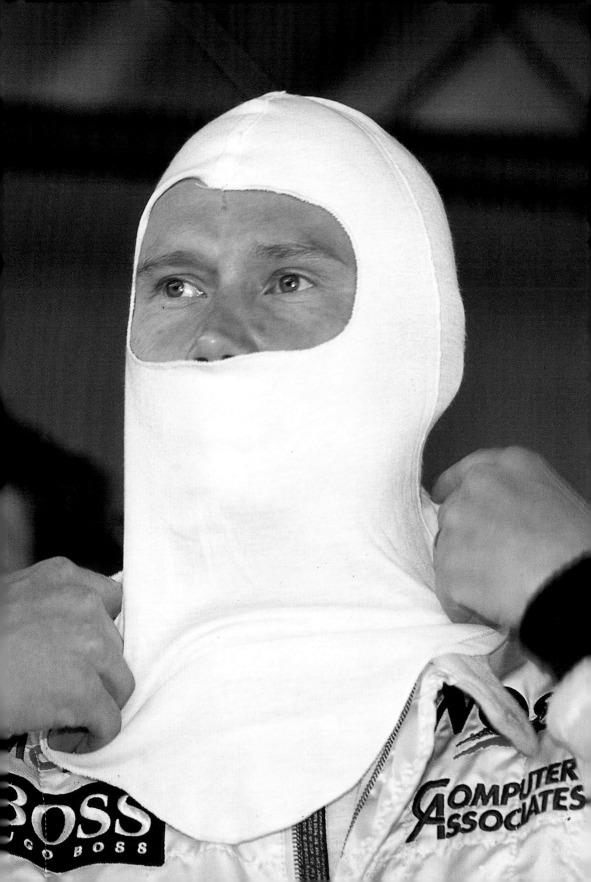

full fitness, to where I was. I've been told to drink a lot, eat a lot of good food, until the point where Professor Watkins says I can start doing exercises. Already I'm using an exercise bike and The Prof has said that if I'm fit enough he is prepared to let me start driving the McLaren again at the end of January.'

In fact, Watkins told Hakkinen that he could move into full training early in January, and he flew to Bali for a couple of weeks where, in the warmth, he could do long beach runs. 'I actually had to stop myself doing too much and harming my muscles.'

On Monday 5 February at the Paul Ricard circuit in the south of France, which McLaren had hired for the occasion, Hakkinen prepared to drive a Formula 1 car again. 'Before going out in the car I was standing next to it, looking around, and I was pretty relaxed. Then I realised the mechanics standing around the car were pretty silent, which is unusual because all the time in Formula 1 something is usually happening. It was completely silent and that was the thing.

In the race he finished fifth, another miracle, and more so as he felt disappointed – 'I came to win'

'I was putting my crash helmet and gloves on and I just started feeling a little bit nervous. As I got in the car and put on the belts I was looking at things, thinking of the past. Nervous is not quite the right word. I was not sure what I was feeling, but when they fired up the engine it sounded great. I selected first gear, went out of the pit lane and everything changed again. It was fantastic. The noise was really nice and the car felt good and I really knew what was going on. I thought *this is great, this is fun, I love it* and I didn't feel scared any more.'

Hakkinen covered a total of 63 laps, including 25 consecutively, and recorded a best time of 1m 07.09s – significantly faster that Schumacher had managed in the Ferrari the day before (1m 07.60s).

An interesting insight from John Alcorn into a racing driver's mind: 'If you have a really big shunt, the next time you get in the car you are always a good second a lap quicker. Why? I don't know, but I think it *almost makes you feel indestructible.* I had a massive shunt testing a Formula 3000 car at Oulton Park once. The left rear tyre let go as I was turning into the double-apex right-hander. I was doing about 140mph

(225kph), flat in fourth. The car ricocheted for about 800 yards back and forth, back and forth. The engine was ripped off the tub and when the car came to rest all that was left was me and the tub. The engine was at the corner before the start-finish straight. After that we went testing at Pembrey and Russell Spence [a promising young driver of the era] was there. We'd tested together before and I'd been about a second and a half slower. Now at Pembrey I was nearly a full second quicker. That was the next time I'd stepped into a car after Oulton.'

Hakkinen flew to Australia for the first race of 1996, Melbourne, and confessed: 'Sitting in an aeroplane when you are over Australia you think this is where you had a big shunt. You have to close the curtains and don't look or think about it. If you do, your emotions can affect you.' In the race he finished fifth: another miracle, and more so because he felt disappointed. 'I came to win. It's a simple thing.' He earned genuine admiration for this 'come-back', although in the strict sense of the words it wasn't that because he hadn't been away. Many people felt that somehow the accident matured Hakkinen, and certainly Martin Brundle was prepared to say so in public.

Hakkinen was now being partnered by David Coulthard. It is true that neither would win a race in 1996, but Hakkinen did score points 11 times and finished fifth in the Championship with 31. The highlight was a third place at Monza: on lap 3 he and Alesi touched, costing Hakkinen a pit stop for a new front wing. He emerged far down the field and put together a long, sustained, superb thrust.

It is also true that 1996 seemed something to be endured, a finite period of time to be got through before the anticipated improvement in 1997; and Melbourne, opening 1997, confirmed this. Coulthard put his McLaren on the second row, Hakkinen on the third but, more important, they were fully on the pace at important moments during the race. Coulthard won, Hakkinen third.

'Of course I'd like to swop places with David,' he said [chuckle], 'but for the team it is fantastic. All the hard work that has been going on in all the testing for years has started paying off and it's just fabulous. I mean, I'm just really happy and a little bit emotional also because it's been a tough time for a long time.'

In Brazil he started on the second row and finished fourth; in Argentina he qualified 17th and worked his way steadily up to fifth, a performance that prompted Rosberg – with not a little pride in his voice – to say, 'He's learning, isn't he? He's driving intelligently, isn't he?' These are entirely rhetorical questions when Rosberg asks them, no confirming 'yes' required.

Interestingly, when I'd been discussing Estoril 1993 with Hakkinen and how hard he had found the racing there, he'd broken the chronological order of the narrative by vaulting to this same Argentina, April 1997, to show exactly how hard. He said: 'To drive the Grand Prix then, and even more now, is so physically demanding that it is unbelievable. It is so bloody heavy. You sit in the same position for what seems like hours turning the wheel, working the pedals and there's the noise, the bumps, there's the other cars to worry about. It's got to be tough and it is tough. After Argentina I was completely knackered. I was *so* tired after that race, it was so hard because I was pushing from start to finish.'

But you're used to it.

'I'm not used to it, but I'm working hard at it. That's the way, physically and mentally, to cope with all that.'

Yes, interesting, because Hakkinen has been in Formula 1 since 1991 and this was his 82nd race. His words bring me back to the Acknowledgements section at the beginning of the book and the questions I was putting that, I could see, puzzled him a bit, namely *what's it really like?* You, Mika Hakkinen, know but the rest of us don't and can barely imagine the full impact of such as Argentina: 1 hour 52 minutes 32.066 seconds with the car, the G-forces and at least one teeth-grinding bump tearing at you every single second and, over the whole of it, you will *average* 101.547 miles per hour (162kph) – because it's a slow track. In Brazil it was 119.251mph (191kph).

I asked him to evaluate the season up to that point and I include his thinking because it illustrates so aptly a great Formula 1 tradition: gut-felt optimism.

'It's never going to be good when you're not leading, not winning. That's where we are so far. Well, let's say David has won one race and I haven't. Anyway, we are still far away from the pace on the lap times we are doing. That's the fact. Then again, looking at last year and the year before, we were further back then on lap times. We are much closer

Right Hakkinen and McLaren boss Ron Dennis working out how to make the team great again (Photo Wilhelm, courtesy Mercedes-Benz).

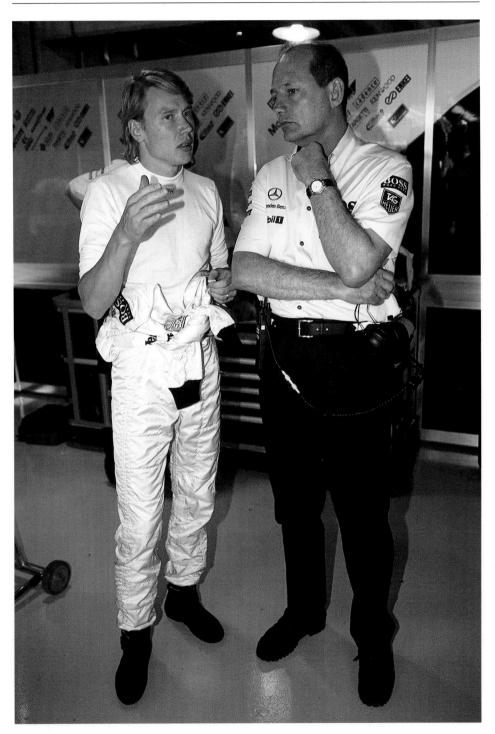

now, very close indeed. I have great chances to be up there at the front later in the season. I've finished in the points in all the first four races.'

You're driving as well as you have ever done.

'Yeah, but I don't look at it that way. I'm thinking about the next race. The team has some new things coming and then I hope we can start winning races. I want to win, I want to win a hell of a lot. If somebody asks me how the season has gone so far, well I'm third in the Championship [on 10 points, after Imola, along with Coulthard, Berger, Heinz-Harald Frentzen and Eddie Irvine], but I haven't been winning. So, for me, disaster, because the car is not quick enough. That's what I feel, that is the feeling that is coming from myself. The fact is, there is an enormous effort from the people behind the team and it's getting closer. A fabulous effort from Mercedes, from Ilmor, from McLaren, from all parties, I have to admit that, but something is still missing. There's something that we haven't got yet . . .'

We're sitting in Rosberg's office, a broad room with trophies and helmets and pictures as ornaments. In a corner there's a proper bar, counter and all, but this is a room for working, definitely not drinking. Even if there are bottles and glasses, they aren't visible. Rosberg always seems to create a mini-whirlwind of activity around himself as he proceeds about his daily business, but he's not here today and a sort of quietness has fallen into the room, broken only when Hakkinen speaks or chuckles so merrily, his face opening to accommodate it. He becomes a boy again then, full of impish delights. [Mustakari says, 'When I think of how he was in 1988 and how he is now, well, he's seen the world and grown into a man but he hasn't changed at all in *who* he is.' It's why he has been popular throughout his career and remains so.]

We've returned from lunch and I have to report that, contrary to everything you have read so far, he not only offered to pay but insisted on paying, no argument. The head waiter, a bustling Italian, nods, but Hakkinen has forgotten to bring any money. Therefore he firmly tells the head waiter he'll pay tomorrow and the head waiter is sympathetic but paying tomorrow would be – well, you know how it is – awkward, got to balance the books and so on. To ease this congestion I paid but, hand on my heart, I insist that he *really did want to pay.*

I couldn't have . . . at my age . . . couldn't have . . . fallen for the Choirboy Syndrome?

Could I?

Mika Hakkinen's career statistics

P = pole position;
FL = fastest lap;
DIS = disqualified;
DNF = did not finish;
DNS = did not start;
JS = penalised for jumping start;
R = retired.

1974–1986
Karting – five times Finnish champion.

1987
Finnish, Swedish and Nordic Formula Ford 1600 champion; also two rounds of the EFDA 1600 Championship and FF Festival (Reynard)

13 Sept	Zandvoort	P/R
27 Sept	Zolder	1
1 Nov	FF Festival, Brands Hatch	R

1988
GM Vauxhall-Lotus Challenge
(Dragon Motorsport/Marlboro)

4 Apr	Thruxton	P/FL/2
17 Apr	Silverstone	1
24 Apr	Donington	FL/2
8 May	Mallory Park	FL/2
29 May	Knockhill	DNF
12 June	Thruxton	FL/4
26 June	Donington	P/FL/JS
10 July	Silverstone	8
11 Sept	Mondello Park	P/FL/1
16 Oct	Thruxton	P/FL/1

Championship: A McNish 142, Hakkinen 127, J. Bell 70

Opel-Lotus Euroseries
(Dragon Motorsport/Marlboro)

19 June	Zandvoort	P/FL/1
2 July	Paul Ricard	P/FL/1
10 July	Silverstone	8
24 July	Hockenheim	FL/4
30 July	Spa	FL/1
7 Aug	Knutstorp	FL/1
21 Aug	Brands Hatch	FL/2
4 Sept	Nurburgring	12
25 Sept	Estoril	13
2 Oct	Jerez	FL/3

Championship: Hakkinen 126, H. Larsen 125, McNish 77

1989
Lucas British Formula 3 except Monaco GP, 6 May (Dragon/Marlboro – Reynard TOM's Toyota), Cellnet F3 Superprix, 22 October (WSR – Ralt-Mugen Honda) and Macau Grand Prix, 26 November

27 Mar	Thruxton	15
9 Apr	Silverstone	DIS

23 Apr	Brands Hatch	P/FL/3
1 May	Silverstone	DNF
6 May	Monaco GP	16
21 May	Brands Hatch	P/2
29 May	Thruxton	12
4 June	Silverstone	19
2 July	Donington	8
15 July	Silverstone	FL/3
6 Aug	Snetterton	5
13 Aug	Oulton Park	6
28 Aug	Silverstone	10
3 Sept	Brands Hatch	6
17 Sept	Donington	DNF
8 Oct	Silverstone	11
15 Oct	Thruxton	12
22 Oct	Brands Hatch	P/FL/1
26 Nov	Macau GP	R

Championship: McNish 72, D. Brabham 56, D. Higgins 48 (Hakkinen seventh, 18)

1990

British Formula 3 (Team WSR/Marlboro; car Ralt-Mugen Honda) except 17 June (Italian F3), 13 October (German F3), 25 November (Macau GP)

1 Apr	Donington	P/FL/1
8 Apr	Silverstone	P/3
16 Apr	Thruxton	P/FL/1
29 Apr	Brands Hatch	P/FL/1
7 May	Silverstone	2
20 May	Brands Hatch	P/FL/2
28 May	Thruxton	FL/2
10 June	Silverstone	P/DNF
17 June	Imola	1
1 July	Donington	6
14 July	Silverstone	2
5 Aug	Snetterton	FL/1
12 Aug	Oulton Park	P/FL/1
27 Aug	Silverstone	P/FL/1
2 Sept	Brands Hatch	P/FL/1
16 Sept	Donington	P/FL/1
23 Sept	Thruxton	2
7 Oct	Silverstone	P/1
13 Oct	Hockenheim	P/FL/1
25 Nov	Macau GP	P/FL/DNF
2 Dec	Fuji	DNQ

Championship: Hakkinen 121, M. Salo 98, S. Robertson 49

1991
Formula 1 (Lotus-Judd)

10 Mar	US, Phoenix	DNF
24 Mar	Brazil, Interlagos	9
28 Apr	San Marino, Imola	5
12 May	Monaco, Monte Carlo	DNF
2 June	Canada, Montreal	DNF
16 June	Mexico, Mexico City	9
7 July	France, Magny-Cours	DNQ
14 July	Britain, Silverstone	12
28 July	Germany, Hockenheim	DNF
11 Aug	Hungary, Budapest	14
25 Aug	Belgium, Spa	DNF
8 Sept	Italy, Monza	14
22 Sept	Portugal, Estoril	14
29 Sept	Spain, Barcelona	DNF
20 Oct	Japan, Suzuka	DNF
3 Nov	Australia, Adelaide	19

Championship: A. Senna 96, N. Mansell 72, R. Patrese 53 (Hakkinen joint 15th, 2)

1992
Formula 1 (Lotus Ford HB)

1 Mar	South Africa, Kyalami	9
22 Mar	Mexico, Mexico City	6
5 Apr	Brazil, Interlagos	10
3 May	Spain, Barcelona	DNF
17 May	San Marino, Imola	DNQ
31 May	Monaco, Monte Carlo	DNF
14 June	Canada, Montreal	DNF
5 July	France, Magny-Cours	4
12 July	Britain, Silverstone	6
26 July	Germany, Hockenheim	DNF
16 Aug	Hungary, Budapest	4
30 Aug	Belgium, Spa	6
13 Sept	Italy, Monza	DNF
27 Sept	Portugal, Estoril	5
25 Oct	Japan, Suzuka	DNF
8 Nov	Australia, Adelaide	7

Championship: Mansell 108, Patrese 56, M. Schumacher 53 (Hakkinen eighth, 11)

1993

Formula 1 (McLaren-Ford HB) except 22 May (Porsche Supercup), 15 Aug (Porsche Supercup)

22 May	Monaco	P/1
15 Aug	Hungaroring	P/FL/1
26 Sept	Portugal, Estoril	DNF
24 Oct	Japan, Suzuka	3
7 Nov	Australia, Adelaide	DNF

Championship: A. Prost 99, Senna 73, D. Hill 69 (Hakkinen joint 15th, 4)

1994

Formula 1 (McLaren-Peugeot)

27 Mar	Brazil, Interlagos	DNF
17 Apr	Pacific, Aida	DNF
1 May	San Marino, Imola	3
15 May	Monaco, Monte Carlo	DNF
29 May	Spain, Barcelona	DNF
12 June	Canada, Montreal	DNF
3 July	France, Magny-Cours	DNF
10 July	Britain, Silverstone	3
31 July	Germany, Hockenheim	DNF
28 Aug	Belgium, Spa	2
11 Sept	Italy, Monza	3
25 Sept	Portugal, Estoril	3
16 Oct	Europe, Jerez	3
6 Nov	Japan, Suzuka	7
13 Nov	Australia, Adelaide	12

Championship: Schumacher 92, Hill 91, G. Berger 41 (Hakkinen fourth, 26)

1995

Formula 1 (McLaren-Mercedes)

26 Mar	Brazil, Interlagos	4
9 Apr	Argentina, Buenos Aires	DNF
30 Apr	San Marino, Imola	5
14 May	Spain, Barcelona	DNF
28 May	Monaco, Monte Carlo	DNF
11 June	Canada, Montreal	DNF
2 July	France, Magny-Cours	7

16 July	Britain, Silverstone	DNF
30 July	Germany, Hockenheim	DNF
13 Aug	Hungary, Budapest	DNF
27 Aug	Belgium, Spa	DNF
10 Sept	Italy, Monza	2
24 Sept	Portugal, Estoril	DNF
1 Oct	Europe, Nurburgring	8
29 Oct	Japan, Suzuka	2
12 Nov	Australia, Adelaide	DNS

Championship: Schumacher 102, Hill 69, D. Coulthard 49 (Hakkinen seventh, 17)

1996

Formula 1 (McLaren-Mercedes)

10 Mar	Australia, Melbourne	5
31 Mar	Brazil, Interlagos	4
7 Apr	Argentina, Buenos Aires	DNF
28 Apr	Europe, Nurburgring	8
5 May	San Marino, Imola	8
19 May	Monaco, Monte Carlo	6
2 June	Spain, Barcelona	5
16 June	Canada, Montreal	5
30 June	France, Magny-Cours	5
14 July	Britain, Silverstone	3
28 July	Germany, Hockenheim	DNF
11 Aug	Hungary, Budapest	4
25 Aug	Belgium, Spa	3
8 Sept	Italy, Monza	3
22 Sept	Portugal, Estoril	DNF
13 Oct	Japan, Suzuka	3

Championship: Hill 97, J. Villeneuve 78, Schumacher 59 (Hakkinen fifth, 31)

1997

Formula 1 (McLaren-Mercedes)

9 Mar	Australia, Melbourne	3
30 Mar	Brazil, Interlagos	4
13 Apr	Argentina, Buenos Aires	5
27 Apr	San Marino, Imola	6
11 May	Monaco, Monte Carlo	DNF
25 May	Spain, Barcelona	7